T0090468

OTHER BOOKS
Presented by Claudia Helt

Listen Carefully, Please!
2022

What Awaits Us…
2022

Love Thy Neighbor
2021

Seeking Our Humanity, Part III
2021

Seeking Our Humanity, Part II
2021

Seeking Our Humanity
2021

The Answer in Action
2021

The Answer Illuminated
2019

The Answer
2018

The Time When Time
No Longer Matters
…Continues…
2018

The Time When Time
No Longer Matters
2016

The Book of Ages
2016

Messages From Within:
A Time for Hope
2011

Messages From The Light:
Inspirational Guidance for Light
Workers, Healers, & Spiritual Seekers
2008

Seeking A Better Me!

Claudia Helt

BALBOA.PRESS
A DIVISION OF HAY HOUSE

Balboa Press books may be ordered through booksellers or by contacting:

Balboa Press
A Division of Hay House
1663 Liberty Drive
Bloomington, IN 47403
www.balboapress.com
844-682-1282

Print information available on the last page.

ISBN: 979-8-7652-4497-5 (sc)
ISBN: 979-8-7652-4496-8 (e)

Library of Congress Control Number: 2023916219

Balboa Press rev. date: 09/07/2023

Welcome, Dear Reader!

You are invited to an adventure of self-discovery. Although this adventure is a solo journey, you may find that it leads you to deeper and more meaningful connections with Self, Others, and More than you presently imagine possible. Perhaps you may find this invitation curious, and maybe it even appears somewhat mysterious; nevertheless, you are sincerely invited to accept this opportunity.

Dear Reader, it is time for you to discover who you really are! Regardless of where you are in your evolutionary development, the time has come for you to proceed. Take a deep breath and simply be with this new reality. You have encountered an invitation that encourages you to become the person you are intended to be. Just let yourself imagine what is unfolding right before your eyes. Somehow, in some way, you and this book, *Seeking A Better Me!* have crossed paths at this particular time in this particular place for a reason that may or may not be known to you.

Curious? Yes. Mysterious? Indeed. A coincidence? Not a chance! Dear Reader, accept the reality that the appearance of this book is a reminder. *Seeking A Better Me!* is more than just a title for a new book. It is a message for all of us! We all need gentle reminders that ground us back into reality, and this message does that.

I want to be a better me! Don't you? Just imagine what can happen if you and I decide to be the people we are meant to be. Seriously, let yourself imagine this idea. We both have more to offer this remarkable life we are living. We both have more to offer this wonderful planet that we are living upon. And we both have more to offer each other and all those others around us to whom we rarely give a moment of our time.

Dear Reader, I truly want to be a better me and I hope you do as well. Shall we take this next bold step together? Let's accept this invitation and become the better people we are intended to be! Hand-in-hand, heart-to-heart, let's do this!

Chapter One

"**A**h, Dear Reader! You are here! Thank you for joining me on this journey to become a better person. I must admit that I am extremely excited about our adventure. Even though this experience is of a singular nature, it is comforting to know that there are others who are also 'here' in this moment participating in the process. You are not alone, Dear Reader. We are not alone!

Perhaps, the most difficult moment of this journey is the first step. It takes courage to make such a commitment…a vow to devote time and energy to delve into the mystery of Self. Not to worry, Dear Friend, you are perfectly capable of managing this task. After all, you are not alone.

Just take a deep breath and be with the moment. You are here for a reason. You are here to create a better You! The chance of a lifetime has come your way, and you deserve this opportunity to experience self-exploration. You and I, and countless others around the planet are all embarking upon an adventure at the same time. We are so fortunate. Together, we are all seeking self-knowledge, self-expansion, and self-empowerment. Each of us is seeking a better "me!"

We are worthy of this opportunity. YOU are worthy of this opportunity, Dear Reader. Yes! Accept this reality!

YOU are worthy of this opportunity. For the sake of Self, Others, and the More with whom you co-exist, you are wise to pursue this remarkable invitation to become the person you are truly meant to be.

Take a brief moment, and breathe this reality into your innermost being. You demonstrate courage by opening this book and engaging with the first chapter. You reveal wisdom by entertaining the idea to seek a better you.

You have only spent a few minutes of your time and already you are exhibiting the goodness within and the potential that lies ahead. Dear Reader, trust what is happening. Trust your Self! The time has come for all of us to face the reality that humankind is in need of an adjustment. Each of us must participate in this transition in our own unique way. The more who participate, the more quickly changes will transpire.

Access your wisdom again Dear Reader and choose to participate in this Project of Change. If you and I, and countless others, actively and wisely choose to become the people we are intended to be, profound changes will occur across the Earth. We will all benefit from this commitment. As said before, do not worry. We are all capable of managing this task.

So, Dear Readers, let us move forward together!

Chapter Two

*W*elcome, to the first step!

> Take a deep breath…
> Enjoy several more deep breaths if you like…
> Allow a moment of silence to overtake you…
> Sit quietly…
>> Enjoy the silence…
>> Do not rush the moment of silence…
> Embrace the Silence…

~Breathe~

Oh, Dear Friend, accept the silence as the gift it truly is, for the silence is your gateway to profound and exquisite change. For those of you who frequently visit the silence, you are aware of the importance of this simple exercise. You can attest to its many benefits, and most likely, you can also elaborate upon its challenges. Simply stated, the art of accessing the silence is definitely worthy of your attention.

In a world that is extremely busy and filled with endless distractions, choosing an alternative that quiets the chaos is a decision founded in wisdom and ancient remembrance.

At some level of awareness, we know that life is more than the noise and commotion that usurps our attention. We know this, and still, the pandemonium is compelling and addictive. Turning one's back on the outside hullabaloo and the inside turmoil is not easy. Unfortunately, this is a reality that we simply must accept, and each of us must also accept that this is not a time to degrade one's self for succumbing to a situation that is pervasive. You are not alone in this misguided behavior. In truth, it is a worldwide crisis.

Obviously, it is not comforting to know that people all over the planet are experiencing these situational disruptions. However, it is fascinating to step back and realize that we, you and I, are capable of facing our issues and making necessary changes that will actually enhance our levels of peacefulness both internally and externally. Indeed these changes are possible, Dear Readers! A few gentle suggestions are provided that hopefully will assist your endeavors. Please expand and personalize this list of goals as your journey progresses.

Improve your focus.
Increase your awareness of your state of mind.
Release your endless mind chatter.
Create a peaceful state.
Gain clarity about your purpose, your reason for being.
Open pathways to change that will enable you to become the better person that you desire to be.

Seeking A Better Me! is a book that opens doors, creates new pathways, and aids you in discovering who your 'Better Me' may actually be. Think about this, Dear Reader. What does a 'Better Me' mean to you? What does your 'Better Me' look like? How does your 'Better Me" express her or his Self? How does your 'Better Me' impact those around you? What type of outreach will your 'Better Me' have? Will your 'Better Me' have a positive influence on those near to you, and perhaps, to the world at large as well? Will your 'Better Me' actually improve the conditions of humankind and the health of planet Earth?

Ponder these questions, Dear Friends, and generate more questions. Record your newfound questions for future visits. These questions are like gem stones that will enhance your imagination, which in turn will expand your possibilities. Explore your options to the fullest, and as you do so, remember your potential is unlimited.

Chapter Three

*Y*our potential is unlimited! Embrace these words for they are a message reminding you of a truth that was long ago forgotten. Accept these words for the message within them is more important that you currently realize.

Your potential is unlimited! For a brief moment, breathe these words in and allow them to touch every cell within your present form. Honor these words with a moment of your time.

Embrace this message.
Accept this message.
Honor this message.

Your potential is unlimited! It is highly unlikely that this is your first encounter with this small, but compelling message. Perhaps you wonder why it is crossing your path again. Some of you may believe that you have sufficiently addressed the issue already. Others may have briefly considered the idea before, and then rushed along not giving the message the attention that it deserved. Regardless of your previous interactions with these simple, but powerful words, the message once again has positioned itself in the middle of your path. Please pause and ask why. Why is this message visiting you again?

⊚

Take a deep breath.
Take several deep breaths.
Embrace this opportunity.
Open your heart to the reality that this message has once again reached out to you. In essence, you are being called.

...PAY ATTENTION...

This is not a coincidence. It is happening for a reason.

⊚

Accept this opportunity.
This is your opportunity for self-exploration.
An invitation has been extended.
You are being encouraged to seek your full potential.
This is a reminder that there is more to come!

⊚

Honor this message.
Trust what is happening!
Trust your Self!
Trust this message!

Your potential is unlimited! Dear Reader, please give this important message the fresh and vigorous attention that it deserves...that YOU deserve. Do not breeze through this moment, quickly glancing at a communiqué that holds significant meaning for you. Challenge the mind that distracts you and delve deeply into the guidance that is offered.

Your potential is unlimited! This is a declaration of your expansive nature that boldly apprises You of your natural gifts. You are ever-evolving, ever-expanding, ever-contributing, and everlasting. In case you haven't noticed, this message is a reminder that you are a remarkable Being that is worthy of your respect. Honor you by giving this reminder the heartfelt consideration that it deserves. It is time, Dear Reader, to allot time for your inward journey.

Grab your prized journal or your preferred device and settle in for a session to explore the mystery of Self.

> Take your deep breaths.
> Access the guidance previously offered.
> Open your heart to facing the suggestions and questions that have been presented.
> Contemplate upon any other ideas that come to mind.
> Record your discoveries.

You can do this! And don't forget, you are not alone in this process. Each of us, who is participating in this book, is seeking a 'Better Me.' So let's wish each other safe travels as we delve more deeply into our innermost being.

Dear Reader, are you ready to continue? The decision is yours. If you wish to continue with your self-exploration, please do so. *Seeking A Better Me!* is intended to accommodate your needs. While you are engaging in your inner work, *Seeking A Better Me!* faithfully waits for you. It is intended to be an assistant, one that is available when you need it, and one that patiently awaits your needs while you pursue the in-depth information that you are seeking.

Presently you may be wondering why your attention has been directed towards the significance of your unlimited potential, and if so, the answer is simple. You would not be here now, engaging with this book, if you were not seeking more. The desire to be a better person is evidence of someone who is seeking more, wanting more, aching for more, all of which exemplifies an individual passionately feeling from within that there is more to life than she or he is presently experiencing. The ache within calls and spurs the desire to want more, even when the more remains an unknown, elusive quality.

Externally, the need to seek for something that is an unknown seems mysterious; however internally, this strong desire ignited by a forgotten memory reaches out to you, calls to you, beseeches you to expand your present experience to greater proportions. Essentially, you are being reminded that your potential is unlimited and that it is time to become more than you are in this moment.

Dear Reader, please do not perceive this information as an insinuation or a sign that you are not living your life correctly. Instead, perceive it as an indication that it is time to advance forward. Remember, you are an ever-evolving Being designed to perpetually expand your possibilities. Typically, the process of maturing, evolving, resting, and continuing operates so smoothly that the precision with which you progress goes without notice. It happens so easily that one does not even recognize that an evolutionary process is actually underway.

However, there are times when an individual becomes rooted in a particular phase of life for a reason that may or may not be known or clearly understood. As a result of this fixation upon a particular moment in time, the person may lose sight of his/her innate propensity for perpetual expansion. Often this time is accompanied by a sense of unrest and uncertainty. When such a situation arises, other opportunities typically unfold that nudge the individual to proceed ahead again. Unfortunately, these so-called 'nudges' may initially be unrecognizable; therefore, it is in your best interest that you pay exceptional attention to those moments when you feel rattled, doubtful, and/or lost. These moments are of extreme importance. Simply stated, these are transitional moments that propel you forward regardless of your clarity in the moment. Just remember, Dear Friend, during these times of confusion and unrest, you are not alone and you are not lost.

So take a few long deep breaths and accept the reality that your present state of confusion is happening for a reason. It is actually here to take you to a place of renewed clarity. Even though it may not seem apparent, all that is needed throughout your transitional experiences will be provided as you continue to explore your unlimited potential while simultaneously seeking the better you that already exists within.

~ B r e a t h e ~

Chapter Four

The beginning of a new chapter always reminds me of long ago, when so many children stories began with the enchanting words, "Once upon a time…" I loved reading those words over and over again. Even now, I hear the words racing through my mind. Goodness, who knew after all these years those four little words could arouse as much anticipation and excitement now as they had decades ago?

I am tempted to do something that may seem odd, but even so, I think it also may be interesting. What if each of us who are participating in this self-discovery project would begin each exploration in a similar manner as did the old stories of the past? What if we would each approach a new upcoming situation with wide eyes, an open heart, and a commitment to embrace everything that unfolds before us? It's a rather clever idea! Just imagine what might happen if you began the next phase of your journey with the same vigor and courage that you did when you opened your children's book and read the engaging words…Once upon a time!

Dear Reader, let your imagination go wild…

Let your imagination go wild! Isn't that an interesting assignment? Think about it, Dear Friend! Sit back, relax, and allow yourself to think about the act of letting your imagination go wild. Actually, before you settle in and embark upon this adventure, you may wish to grab your supplies. Journal, favorite pen, paintbrush, color pencils, laptop, cup of tea, candles, chocolate, etc.! Whatever is necessary for this undertaking; gather it quickly before you lose your momentum.

Now, let's begin again! Settle in, take your deep breaths, and remember you are not alone on this excursion to discover the wonders of your imagination. In your mind's eye envision all the other readers, who are presently joining you on this potentially self-defining experience. Allow yourself to feel the comfort of their presence.

As you take your deep breaths...
Your companions execute similar efforts.

As you quiet your mind...
They attempt the same.
As you seek individually...
So, too do all who are present.
Take comfort in this camaraderie...
You are not alone.

Step deeper into the quiet...
Make any adjustments that are needed...
You are the orchestrator of this exploration...

Allow your imagination to wander...
Observe where it takes you...
Give it full rein...
Continue to listen and observe...
Mentally note the highlights of your mind's wanderings.
Repeat these simple steps as long as desired...

Discern when it is time to end the exploration process...
Gently, gratefully, and lovingly close the session...
Then gather up your preferred tool/s and take time to elaborate and expound upon your experience.

~ B r e a t h e ~

Take another deep breath as you quietly envision applauding yourself. You have taken another step forward and that is commendable. As you review your experience, open your heart to all that transpired. Leave negative commentary aside, please. It has no place in these sacred moments.

Simply accept what unfolded and marvel at the meanderings of your imagination. It is an incredible gift, is it not? Just imagine what your imagination might be if it functioned under your leadership. Ponder this, Dear Friend, and please give this suggestion considerable attention. After all, you are the leader of your Self, or at least you are intended to be. Envision what your imagination might accomplish if you intentionally accepted the auspicious position as its leader.

While you continue considering this possibility, there is more to be said about the magnificent imagination that accompanied you at the time of your beginning. You and your imagination have been traveling together for a very long time, Dear Friend. Yours is not a new relationship, but one which is of ancient beginnings. This is brought to your attention now, because the time has come for you and your Old Friend to become reacquainted.

If your head is spinning from this surprising news, please be at peace. There is no reason for alarm or unrest. You are simply meeting a Friend from the past, who has accompanied you for a very long time. Even though this transpired without your awareness, the underlying relationship that you share still exists to this day.

Hopefully, some of you may have already discovered this everlasting friendship. If so, this news will not be new to you; however, if this is your present situation, then you are one who can attest to the wonders that can be discovered in the silence. I hope you will do so! Your honesty may pave the way for others to speak their truths as well.

I am one who personally believes that many, many people across the planet are aware of an awe-inspsiring connection that is shared with an indescribable other. My reason for believing this comes without valid documentation; however my experiences are evidence that perpetuate my beliefs. Initially, I was totally taken aback by the unusual encounters that seemingly appeared out of nowhere, and which quickly became an everyday occurrence. Like many before me, I was afraid to speak about my unusual interactions with the unknown other.

After all, hearing voices, having visions, and participating in automatic writing were not behaviors that gained accolades in my profession. As a Licensed Professional Counselor, I was convinced that sharing my experiences with colleagues would not be a wise choice. Not only would such an interaction put my license and career in jeopardy, but it would also have placed my colleagues in a very awkward situation. Fearful for myself and also for them, I remained silent about these experiences for what seemed a very long time. Years later, I now know that I was not the only person having these unusual experiences, but few of us were willing to speak of this at the time because we were afraid of the ramifications that might occur.

It is most unfortunate that throughout history, many have felt and believed it was necessary to hide these truths about our personal experiences. Sadly, such concerns are still warranted. Many suffered for remembering and speaking the truths in the past, and as a result, those of today have become extremely cautious about discussing matters that can reveal the essence of who we really are.

This is an issue that may arise for those who seek a 'Better Me.' Each of you may develop in ways that may be surprising, and unusual events may cause you to question your process. What is happening? Why is it happening? How is it happening? Who is responsible for these mysterious happenings? This is a common reaction when one begins to expand his or her awareness of existence. Just allow yourself to be openhearted and curious to whatever is happening.

There will be times when one is so excited about the new burgeoning experiences that he or she may wish to share everything that is occurring with everyone encountered. These moments of fullness and joy truly are transformative. Some may feel these transitions as large and expansive occasions, while others may experience their circumstances as quiet, serene events that also seem remarkably expansive and seemingly unimaginable. The truth is all experiences are different and equally significant. Remember this please: all experiences are equally significant.

Because the human species is inclined towards competitiveness, it is essential that each of us embrace everyone's experiences with equal openheartedness and respect. Competitive attitudes are distracting and disruptive. They serve no purpose in this discovery process. If you truly wish to seek and become a 'Better Me,' you must direct your efforts with kindness and compassion. Ah, Dear Friends, this is another truth that is in our best interest to remember. In seeking a 'Better Me,' we must at all times, in all occasions direct our efforts from a place of kindness and compassion.

It is time to pause for another moment of deep breathing. Please accept this opportunity to relax for a few moments. Those of you who are inclined to speed through this resting experience, please check in with yourself. Why would you decline an opportunity for deep breathing and resting?

~Breathe~

Throughout *Seeking A Better Me!* you will be invited, advised, and strongly encouraged to practice pausing and taking deep breaths. There is a reason for this. As one's life becomes increasingly busier with whatever life circumstances are yours to manage, the natural breathing rhythm of the human form diminishes. It happens without our notice, but wisdom tells us to be alert to this situation.

Please take advantage of these opportunities to enhance and enjoy your personal breathing process. Your efforts will revitalize your natural breathing rhythm; and then extend these breathing exercises into a practice that you can incorporate into a daily routine. Giving attention to this simple task is a gift to your Self. Take another deep breathe now for good measure.

Dear Friends, we began this chapter with a reminder of times past when we were young and enamored with the beginning of the children's books that were read to us, and later, those that we read ourselves. 'Once upon a time' awakened us to the possibilities that there was more, and those four words have the same influence upon us to this day.

Once upon a time we came into existence and it was more than we ever imagined. The lust to explore all the amazing possibilities propelled us forward for a time, but at some point, most of us became distracted by life's circumstances. The dreams, the imaginations that excited us grew dim. Some of us maintained the spark of possibility, some didn't, but the reality of those possibilities still exists. The opportunity for exploration and discovery still exists. Once upon a time, our imaginations were powerful, creative, and filled with possibilities that today still exist. Imagine that! Yes, imagine that and open your heart to pursuing that which you thought was lost. Once upon a time, you knew that you were more than you appeared to be. You were right! You were more then, and you still are today.

Think about this! And ask the question that is blatantly obvious and necessary. What are you going to do about this?

Regardless of where you are in your personal journey, there is more for you to discover. You would not be reading this book if you didn't sense this truth from within.

If you are dissatisfied with where you are at this moment, then what are you going to do to change your situation? If you are satisfied with your present circumstances, what are the next steps to be taken? Regardless of where you are in your evolutionary development, there is more waiting for you to discover about you, about others, about Everything!

Dear One, there is more to this life that you are presently living than you can possibly imagine. It is time for you and the imagination that has accompanied you since your beginning to reunite again. It is time for you to merge into the state of Oneness that has always been available to you, but which was momentarily forgotten. It is time to discover who you really are now in this moment, and it is time to seek the 'Better Me' that you are, have always been, and will always be.

Chapter Five

***B**egin* this chapter with another deep breath. We are beginning another adventure, and every adventure demands a deep breath. Enjoy several more, if you will, allowing your breath to realign with the rhythm of your body and the Earth herself.

~ B r e a t h e ~

Dear Reader, who are you now in this very moment? Please be with this question and observe where your mind takes you. Take notes, please! Much will be learned from observing your mind. Simply be with the question. Who are you now in this very moment?

Face whatever transpires with an open heart. Do not shy away from your present findings. Simply observe what is surfacing without dread, fear, or shame. However, if those feelings arise, embrace them! Record each observation boldly. Do not deny these realities and do not try to hide from them. What we attempt to hide remains with us for extended periods of time. In essence, trying to hide the unwanted aspects of one's life expends great amounts of time and energy that could be focused on other more promising possibilities.

Dear Reader, a gentle reminder is necessary. The journey to seek a 'Better Me' is your personal discovery process. What arises during this exploration process is between you and You! The work that you pursue is for the betterment of you. Be bold! Be courageous! Be openhearted! Be honest with yourself!

Sometimes the brave soul that begins this type of work is halted by the fear that secrets will surface that she or he does not want to be known by anyone else, including a Higher Source that is relevant to that particular person. It is not uncommon for individuals to refrain from going further into their self-discovery process because of their fear that this Higher Source will be displeased with the secrets.

Another gentle reminder: The Higher Source already knows all of our secrets. And this Higher Source is absolutely delighted that we are engaging in this important inner work. Please release your fears of being judged. That character trait is human bound not celestial.

Everything you observe throughout this exploration process is part of who you are at this moment in time. Accept the truth of what is unfolding before you and express gratitude for your discoveries and for what lies ahead.

So, again the question is: Who are you now in this very moment? Quickly jot down everything that comes forward. These precious thoughts are the foundation from which more information will be gathered later.

Typically, when a profound question is asked, there is an explosive thought response. So much is provided instantaneously that it is difficult to consume all the information at once. And too often, something is highlighted that may capture one's attention at the expense of all the other information that is equally important. Humans are easily distracted, particularly by thoughts or memories that trigger us. Once that occurs, it is a battle to stay focused. We become engulfed in an incident that overpowers all the other aspects of our lives, which redirects the intent of the question.

The question regarding who we really are is expansive and never-ending. We can spend the rest of our life expounding upon it, and in many ways we do, by repeatedly reassessing where we are and who we are as we move along our journey of life. This is all part of the seeker's adventure. Our curiosity about who we are and why we are here is a constant.

Seeking A Better Me! is intended to focus the Reader on the here and now. It is a given that we are constantly changing, so let's accept that truth, and direct our focus upon this moment in time. Who are you now in this very moment?

Let's restate this, Dear Reader, especially for you. You may choose if you are so inclined, to read the rest of this paragraph out loud. Who am I in this very moment? How can I lovingly and healthily pursue the answers to my question? How can I practice self-care as I seek and discover answers that may or may not please me? How can I gently, compassionately adjust to and accept the answers that are discovered? How can I consciously and tenderly learn from this information, thereby creating the 'Better Me' that I am seeking?

Dear Reader, you are who you are, and because you are who you are, you are seeking to improve yourself. This is your way of being. Although this truth may momentarily escape you, it remains the truth forevermore. *Seeking A Better Me!* is a reminder that you are who you are…a precious Being filled with unlimited potential and endless desire to become more than you presently are in this moment. Understanding that this is part of your genetic makeup may encourage you to accept the reality that you are indeed a special Being. For those of you who have difficulty accepting compliments, be at peace. This is not a compliment; it is simply the reality of your circumstances. Rather than battling with this reality, you may instead choose to accept it as an essential part of who you are and recognize that this truth is also an essential part of who you are becoming. Breathe deeply, Dear Reader, and allow this information to reach every cell within you.

~ B r e a t h e ~

Once again, continue to enjoy your deep breathing exercises. This simple exercise not only extends your stamina and enhances your vitality, but it also freshens the soul. The importance of maintaining one's natural rhythm of breathing deserves much more attention. We began this chapter by taking a deep breath before engaging upon a new adventure. The adventure continues, as all of the Readers who are seeking a 'Better Me' prepare to take the next step.

Dear Friends, it is time for each of you to align your Self with the One within you. Although this may sound strange to some of you, please relax into the process. You are not alone. Your Companions on this journey are here. Each of you will find your own unique way of relaxing, quieting your mind, and merging into the silence. There is no correct way of attaining this goal. It simply develops with patience, commitment, desire, persistence, and trust.

The next step, as you well know, is to delve more deeply into the question previously discussed. "Who are you at this moment in time?"

This is your moment in time to willingly and purposefully seek more information about your Self. If you find that you are not able to pursue this endeavor at this moment, then honor your other commitments and also discern a time frame that will work for you and mark it on your calendar. If you do not have other commitments, but are resisting this exercise, then change the question. Instead ask, "Why are you allowing this opportunity to pass you by?"

One must be honest with oneself, Dear Reader. There are times when we are filled with energy to pursue our inner work, and there are times when for a variety of reasons, we are not. Remember, you are the leader of your journey. Do what you need to do, but be honest with yourself. Do you really need to attend other matters, or are you having doubts about pursuing this process. These questions are important. If you are not committed to the work at this time, then do not waste your time. But do challenge your Self! If not now, when?

Dear Friend, you are here for a reason! Slow down, and give yourself time to discover why you are avoiding discovering who you really are. We, all of us, hope you will join us today, as we leap into the Silence, but if not, rest assured you are still in our hearts and you are welcome to join us at any time. The journey of self-discovery is an ongoing process. You will know when the time is right. In the meantime, we wish you safe travels and peace of mind.

Now, Dear Friends, those of you who are up for this exercise, let us begin again. Take another deep breath and focus your intentions upon the deepening process.

Breathe deeply at a pace that is satisfying and comforting.
Relax into the rhythm that is developing.
Enjoy the sacred moment that is unfolding.
Accept the sweet beauty of this moment.
Be in peace.

From this place of serenity, listen with the ears of your heart.
Listen to your breath…inhaling…exhaling…
    Listen to the Silence.
    Practice patience.
In the Silence resides another.
    Sometimes heard; sometimes not…
    In patience be; it is the way to connection.

Remain as you are...
  waiting for the Silence to consume you...
Leading you deeper and deeper to the space
  where connection awaits you.
You need not search for this connection,
  it surrounds you.
That which you seek is Everywhere,
  waiting quietly, patiently for the moment
  when you will welcome it home.
Rest, Dear Friend.
  Open your heart...
  Release all thoughts...
  Breathe naturally, slowly, rhythmically.
Rest, Dear Friend.
  Be still...
  Be accepting...
  Be at peace.
Remain comfortable in the Silence
  as long as you desire.

Discern when you are ready to continue.
Address the topic in question.
Who are you at this moment in time?
  Speak the truth about your Self...
  This is a private conversation...
    Face your fears.
    Do not hide from your Self.

Focus on your positive attributes first.

Elaborate upon your goodness.

Celebrate your achievements.

Accept who you are!

Acknowledge the parts of you that require improvement.

Be honest with your Self.

Do not hide from this side of you.

Be with this side of you, and take the next step.

Mindfully make amends for your behavior.

From within, express your necessary apologies…

From within, express your commitments to change…

From within, express your forgiveness to your Self.

Breathe deeply and celebrate your achievements.

Accept this side of you. Accept your Self!

Be with who you are at this moment in time.

Spend time getting to know you.

Do so with grace, compassion, love, and optimism.

Simply be with you.

The next step awaits you.

Dear One, feel good about your Self. The inner work that you just accomplished is noteworthy. Few have the courage to do what you just did. Few have the courage to face who they really are. Applaud yourself, and give yourself time to adjust to your new discoveries. Please open your heart to 'all of you.' If you are like most humans, this exercise will reveal attributes that please you and others that will not. All of this information is equally important and it requires time to digest.

As you continue your inner work regarding what was just discovered, please be kind to yourself. This is no time for harsh negative commentary, nor is it time to ignore that which was difficult to review. Visit both ends of the continuum that comprise who you are. Learn more about the best of you and also about the worst of you. All aspects of who you are demand your attention. You are a wealth of information from which great gains can be made. Be gentle with yourself as you discern how you wish to proceed from here. After all, the goal is to seek to be a 'Better Me!'

Please take this project seriously. You deserve this tender, careful attention. It's important. You're important. Also there is another suggestion that you will hopefully consider and incorprate into your daily routine.

Enjoy This Process!

Even though it can be complicated at times, enjoy what you are doing. You are making progress. Be happy about that! This work has the potential for great change in your life. Enjoy and respect what you are doing for YOU!

Chapter Six

Seeking A Better Me! was created to be an assistant in your journey to discover who you really are. Like all good assistants, the book is intended to play many roles in your life. As you pursue your self-exploration process, your assistant nudges you forward, inspiring you to think and live more expansively. At times your assistant invites you to take another step forward, but never are you forced to do so. With each new step, you are reminded that you are not alone. Others are with you, and you are with others. The camaraderie is reassuring and gratifying. When your assistant senses your need for rest, you are guided in that direction. You are urged frequently to take deep breaths, to pause, and to relax when necessary throughout all the inner work that you are encouraged to participate in. While *Seeking A Better Me!* is intended to be a good assistant, you are intended to be the leader of your self-exploration adventure. Dear Reader, you have authority over your journey of exploration and expansion at all times.

Obviously, each individual who participates in this 'seeking experience' enters the process with his or her unique set of circumstances. Likewise, each of you will have your own unique reactions to whatever is personally discovered. Hopefully, all of you will seek the support and guidance that is provided in *Seeking A Better Me!* as you brave your way through this transformative undertaking.

One of the purposes of this unique book is that it is a means for revealing truths that are truths for everyone. Since we are all so uniquely different, this comment may sound doubtful. Nevertheless, we must remember that we are also all uniquely One, and this statement regarding Oneness is one of the many truths that is a truth for all. Many other truths, which are also universal truths, will be discovered during your inward journey. As you encounter these wondrous phenomena, there will be factors that need to be taken into consideration. Timeliness is one of those factors.

For instance, what is read today may be perceived differently if read tomorrow. A message that arrives before one is ready to receive it may not be useful to the individual in the moment; however, as time passes and circumstances change, the message when encountered again can become profoundly influential to his or her development. Remember this please as you access this book throughout your journey. Use it when you need it, and be a free spirit when you feel so guided. Hopefully, *Seeking a Better Me!* has already assisted you with your seeking expedition, and I truly hope it will continue to be of assistance, but remember your authority remains within you. That authority brought you to this point in time. Continue to access that important part of you whenever it is needed during your exploration process.

Another factor that deserves consideration during your self-discovery experience is the reality that you are not alone on this adventure. You purposefully were introduced to the idea of honoring your fellow readers as special companions during this exploration adventure. Through this visionary process, a community with whom you can feel connection has been created. This sense of connection with the other Readers is both comforting and warm-hearted. Overtime, they become your friends as you delve more deeply into your seeking process. You come to accept that these new friends are with you in heart, but not in presence, and the heartfelt connection is profoundly gratifying.

Just as you have these, shall we call them, long-distant assistants, so too do you have other assistants, nudging you along the way. These helpers are constantly watching over you, attempting to bring experiences forward that you desire to encounter. Although you may not remember that these experiences were of your own design, your companions do. They abide by the sacred contract that was agreed to long ago. Their efforts usually go unnoticed; however, the commitments made by these friends of old are stellar and worthy of your attention.

As you progress forward, you may choose to be more open minded to situations that just seem to happen in a coincidental manner. If you hear yourself saying that something was a coincidence, <u>pay attention</u> to the incident. Explore what transpired and ponder the amazing events that occurred around you. These so-called coincidences are actions that were carefully provided on your behalf. Once you start paying attention to these incidents, you will have a much greater understanding of the reality that you live in. You are not alone. You have many companions who are assisting you in ways that sometimes feel miraculous.

Enjoy this reality! Accept it! And also remember that your authority over your journey is still real and it still exists.

Some of you, Dear Readers, may feel as if someone other than yourself is in charge of your life. When that happens, <u>pay attention</u>. Give credence to the reality that something truly may be going on, even though it is seemingly operating without your will or intention. It is in your best interest to explore such experiences, even if you do not feel you are benefitting from the event. Again, please heed this suggestion. <u>Pay attention!</u> Please excuse this repeated bit of advice, but paying attention is an instrumental aspect of your growth process that enhances your ability to be consistently more present, which in turn increases your awareness of what is transpiring in every moment. Explore these situations fully so that you can revel in the support that was initiated for you.

On the other hand, if you feel someone truly is interfering with your process, <u>pay attention</u> to that as well. There are times when it seems as if another is disrupting our process, making us feel as if we are being controlled by another. This is rarely the case. Typically, these interferences that take us away from our good intentions are actually normal, everyday distractions of life. These distractions can be insidious, cleverly capturing our attention and convincing us that their needs must immediately be attended. The process can unfold with the blink of an eye, and unfortunately, can sustain itself for long periods of time. In essence our lack of attention is perpetuated by our lack of attention. Not to worry, Dear Friends. You are not alone in this annoying pattern. Most of us tend to frequent this path on a regular basis. Fortunately, it is a habit that can be monitored and overcome.

Actually, much can be learned from the distractions that demand so much of our attention. Even though our distractions can be very disruptive, they do offer important information about the Self. Rather than battling with these distractions that cause us tremendous frustration, it would be wise to study the underlying messages that are embedded in these repeated and persistent patterns. Perhaps these repetitive experiences are happening for a reason.

Please remember, Dear Friend, an essential part of our journey entails discernment. Acquiring more knowledge about your attention skills, or lack thereof, is an opportunity to learn more about the Self, thereby also learning how to take better care of your Self.

Another factor that is extremely important to your self-discovery process is the willfulness of your mind. Although you as an individual have authority over your journey, the mind mistakenly believes it is in control of all aspects of your life. For those of you who are inclined to highlight or underline important points that are particularly relevant, please prepare yourself for the next statement. Your mind is not in control of your life! This is a critically important reality that must be dealt with, so let's repeat this message. **Your mind is not in control of your life!** It is, however, an exquisite companion that can assist you in countless ways when it is guided by your leadership. Please highlight the previous statement, as well.

Because the mind's role is significantly important in your understanding of your own authority, let's pursue an exercise that will assist you in exploring your relationship with your mind.

✺

Begin with several deep breaths.
Find a pace that is just right for you.
Eyes can be opened or closed…your choice.
Allow your body to relax and open your heart to new discoveries.
Another deep breath, please.

✺

Now, quiet your mind.
Nothing more is requested, just move into a state of quietness.
Allow a minimum of 15 minutes for this part of the exercise.
Observe your mind, but refrain from taking notes please.
Just notice your mind's patterns.
Request your mind to return to a quiet state, if necessary.
Restrain from critical comments and judgments.
Enjoy another deep breath when you have completed the exercise.

✺

Take time to record your observations.
Be diligent. Be precise. Be expansive.
This is a precious opportunity to strengthen your relationship with your mind.
Were you able to quiet your mind?
For how long?

Was it easy to achieve?

Was it difficult?

Was your mind active during the exercise?

How did your mind respond when you requested it to return to a state of being quiet?

Did it respond quickly or did it ignore you?

Did it meander about from topic to topic?

Did it focus upon a particular topic?

Did you eventually lose sight of the exercise?

When you finished the exercise:

What were you thinking?

What were you feeling?

Did you have insights about your experiences?

Did you have concerns about your experiences?

Did you feel connected or disconnected to the exercise?

Take a deep breath, please.

Breathe into your recent experience.

Allow yourself to relax.

Applaud yourself for the effort you made.

Once again, observe what is happening now.

Pay attention to your mind's actions.

Notice what the mind is up to.

Is it working with you or against you?

Gather more information.

Accept what you discover with gratitude.

~ B r e a t h e ~

Dear Reader, welcome back from your adventure. Hopefully, you have learned more about your relationship with your incredible mind. Please feel good about yourself! Few people have done what you just did. Think about that for a moment, because it is a sad truth. Most people never pay any attention to the workings of their mind. It never occurs to them to do so. Having just had this experience, perhaps you now understand how important it is to be aware of the behavior of your mind.

Once again, let me remind you that you have authority over your life, and one of the ways you can demonstrate that authority is by taking good care of yourself. Learning more about the unnoticed escapades of your mind is an excellent example of self-care.

One might think that this is a simple task to accomplish, but in truth, the mind that prefers its own way is extremely resistant to changes that are not of its liking. It may seem odd to discuss the mind as if it is separate from you. Indeed, it is an unusual concept: however, you truly cannot appreciate the reality of this dynamic until you actually spend time studying the operational patterns of your mind. To fully understand the extent of your mind's remarkable capabilities requires significant observation. This is not a one-time event.

Initially, you may be taken aback by the behaviors of your independently thinking mind. As said before, few of us give the mind little if any attention. We simply take it for granted. Nevertheless, the mind has a huge influence upon us whether we are aware of it or not. Needless to say, it is in our best interest to learn as much as we can about the workings of the mind. A few questions that come to mind for me include: how does the mind influence me without my awareness? Is the influence positive or negative? Is the mind assisting me or impeding me? Who is in charge? Is the mind directing me or am I directing my mind? Please feel free to add as many questions to this list as you need to assist your examination of the effects that your mind has upon you. Dear Reader, you and I, and all our companions who are seeking to improve ourselves, must open our hearts to the importance of this self-examination task. No one else can do this for us.

So prepare your Self! It's time to have another encounter with your mind. Do so with a smile on your face and joy in your heart. Envision this image, please. The mind is a remarkable gift, beautifully packaged and wrapped with colorful paper and silky ribbons. And it's waiting for you to open it up and discover all its secrets.

~ B r e a t h e ~

◎

Embrace the opportunity to practice your deep breathing.
Find a pace and rhythm that is suitable for you.
Enjoy this process; it is yours to finesse.
Mastering this act of self-care is an achievement in itself.

◎

Settle into the quiet state that you have created.
Acclimate yourself to the mystery and the beauty of the quiet.

Enjoy the quiet without expectations.
Simply be in the quiet.

Continue adjusting to this wonderful state of serenity.
Manage your rhythmic breathing:
Make any adjustments that are necessary.
Notice any changes that may occur.
Observe the changes without judgment.
Embrace whatever transpires.
Continue observing the changes that are unfolding.

Assess your ability to maintain the silence.
Are you reacting to your environment?
If so, attempt to release the distractions.
Observe what happens without judgment.
Are you reacting to your mind's activity?
Notice the mind's behavior.
Invite the mind to quiet itself.
Observe what happens without judgment.
If necessary, repeat your invitation.
Observation of results is essential.
Assess the tenacity of the mind's will.
Reassure the mind that it is critically important to the success of this exercise.
Invite your mind to cooperate with you.
Observe what happens without judgment.

Return to your breathing exercises.

Relax again.

Regain your sense of peace.

Take time to make notes about your experience.

Elaborate upon the discoveries you made.

How did your mind operate?

Did it assist your intentions or interfere with your intentions?

Was your mind able to maintain focus or did it meander about?

Did your mind follow your lead or did it follow its own accord?

Was your mind willful and determined to have its own way?

Was your mind curious about your preferences?

Was your mind interested and willing to cooperate with your intentions?

Expand upon this list of questions as needed.

Accept the relationship that you presently have with your mind, including the blessings and the challenges.

Wholeheartedly welcome the opportunities for healing and expanding this relationship.

Celebrate the opportunities that lie ahead for you and your mind!

Express your gratitude for this remarkable gift.

~ B r e a t h e ~

Congratulations! You are in the process of creating a better relationship with your mind. Good for YOU! And good for your Mind! Both of you will benefit from this effort. Separately, each of you functions well, but when in unison, your efficiency will be substantially improved and recognizable as an increase in production and a decrease in fatigue. In essence, you and your mind will become a highly skillful and competent team.

We began this chapter by acknowledging that *Seeking A Better Me!* was intended to serve as an assistant to your self-discovery process. The exercises provided in this chapter are merely suggestions that can be used when needed. They are gentle reminders to aid you along the way; however, as you continue exploring more about your Self, you will discover and create your own specialized exercises. Your experiences will be your guide. Patience and perseverance will also enhance your endeavors, as you and your mind naturally learn how to work in unison.

Rest assured, Dear Friend, the efforts exerted in this process will greatly assist you in the days ahead. Having a mind that works with you rather than against you expands your possibilities and heightens your potential for achieving the goals that you are seeking.

Chapter Seven

Dear Reader, it is time to embrace another aspect of *Seeking A Better Me!* In order to do this, you must first accept the truth that you already are the one whom you seek. Before you start rolling your eyes or having diminishing thoughts, please take a deep breath.

Once upon a time, long before you can remember, you came into existence as an indescribable example of perfection. You began in that magnificent way and today, you still are that wonderful Life Being that is ever-growing, ever-expanding, and ever-evolving into yet another better version of your Self. This is who you truly are! Because of your everlasting way of being, it is only natural that you are here now reading a book called *Seeking A Better Me!* Some would say this is serendipitous, while others might prefer the word coincidence, but neither of these descriptors adequately expresses the significance of what is transpiring in this moment of your life. What is happening, Dear Reader, is happening for a reason.

Please accept that the sense of urgency that surfaces from within you is real. The need to understand more about yourself is also real, and it is compounded by an intense desire to be more than you presently seem to be. These are not quirky happenstances. They are innate traits calling to you, reminding you that once again it is time to move forward.

Actually, you have moved forward many times before in this lifetime and in others as well. The memories of these experiences are long forgotten. Even so, a distant familiarity remains deep within you that identifies with what you are experiencing now in the present. The unrest you experience today was experienced before. And it is as real today as it was long ago. It is real! It is not an aberration, Dear Friend, nor is it anything to fear. The agitation that you currently experience is the result of your genetic pattern informing you that you are ready for a new phase of being. Revel in this moment.

For those of you who do not feel that you are ready for a new phase of being, take a deep breath. The fact that you are reading this book insinuates that you are ready for a new experience. However, if you are absolutely certain that you are not ready at this moment, then put the book down for now. Remember, you have authority over your adventure. If you do not want to continue at this time, then honor that decision by taking a break.

On the other hand, if you are unsure about this new possibility, then take another deep breath. Take several, if needed, and gently remind your Self that it is common for uncertainty and anxiety to rise when change is on the horizon. Be that as it may, perhaps this is a time to challenge the doubts that are troubling you. If old habits are interfering with your present decision-making process, consider another option. Rather than embracing an old pattern that may be related to worriment, you might choose to redefine this situation. Maybe the unsettled feelings that you are experiencing are actually excitement. Think about that! Seriously, please give this careful consideration. Many of us are burdened by old patterns that drive us in directions that we are not intended to take, but the habit is so strong that we simply go along with it.

Now, as you contemplate upon how to proceed with your adventure to become a better person, it is time to reflect upon who you are in this moment.

~ B r e a t h e ~

Silence the mind…
> Once again, begin with your breathing regimen.
> With each inhale invite peace of mind.
> With each exhale release that which is not needed.
> Continue the process…in…out…in…out…
>> For as long as is necessary.

Focus your intentions upon who you are…
Visit the aspects of you with which you are satisfied.
> Breathe into each detail: accept who you are.
> Express your gratitude for these positive attributes.

Visit the aspects of you with which you are disappointed.
> Breathe into each detail: accept who you are.
> Express your gratitude for what you have learned.

Visit the aspects of you that are in need of improvement.

Breathe into each detail: accept who you are.

Express your gratitude for what is yet to come.

Revisit what you discovered...

Release sadness, regrets, and heartaches that continue to linger.

Truly accept all aspects of your Self.

Express your appreciation for who you have been, who you are, and who you are yet to be.

Breathe deeply.

Focus your intentions upon who you desire to be...

Create your wish list.

Visit the list daily.

Revise the list as you gain more and more clarity.

Devise a plan for actualizing the changes you wish to make.

Practice your new ways of being daily.

Review your behavior frequently.

Assess your progress and initiate any changes that are needed.

Have patience with this transformational process.

Embrace every new day with an open heart and mind.

Praise your progress and focus on forward motion.

Accept your disappointments without harsh commentary.

Strategize and initiate alternative ways for achieving goals.

Proceed with your new plans.

Celebrate life every day.

Express your appreciation for all that is unfolding daily.

Create a gratitude journal and address it regularly.

Live life fully every day.

Make joy a priority.

Spread love to All you encounter.

Let kindness lead the way.

Have compassion for your efforts and be hopeful for tomorrow.

In your mind, be peaceful.

In your heart, be peaceful.

In your spirit, be peaceful.

Be peaceful every day, every moment, for all days to come.

~ B r e a t h e ~

Thank you, Dear Friend, for your participation in this exercise. Before ending this chapter, spend a few moments imagining what your life would be like if you continued engaging with this exercise on a regular basis. It's breathtaking, isn't it? Just imagine how life will be if you choose to pursue being the better person that you are destined to be.

And then, let's all imagine what life will be like if each one of us who is reading *Seeking a Better Me!* also continues engaging in this transformational process. Just imagine! You and I and all our companions can make the choice to be a better person. We can change the energy of our planet by making this important decision. The opportunity lies before us. We can do this! One by one, people across the planet can choose to become a better person. Just thinking about this makes you shiver with excitement.

As you rest in bed tonight, Dear Friend, remember what you did today. Remember that you participated in an exercise which can change your life and the lives of others.

Don't forget this experience!

This is an opportunity, a personal commitment to your Self that demands your attention. Just in case tomorrow is a busy day for you, let's create a reminder that will bring your attention back to this exercise. The truth is, we are human! And if we lay this book aside even for a day, the chance of forgetting this significant experience is high. Let's choose to avoid that possibility. Remember, we are trying to create a new way of being.

So before you close your book today, Dear Reader, please do one more activity that will hopefully keep you on track. Insert a large marker of some kind that will attract your attention tomorrow, and boldly remind you that this last exercise must be engaged with again.

Thank you, Dear Friends! This is an important day for all of us.

Chapter Eight

*T*hank you, Dear Readers, for continuing. It brings me great pleasure to know that each of you is living into your commitment to become a better person. Your efforts individually and collectively inspire me to continue!

Let's take a few minutes to embrace the importance of inspiration in our lives. I hope you are one who has enjoyed inspirational moments throughout your lifetime, but if this has not been the case, then let me offer you an inspirational thought.

It is never too late!

Please take this message to heart, for it is another truth that applies to everyone. We all require inspiration to enrich our lives. It is as necessary to our well being as is the food we consume on a daily basis. So vitally important is inspiration to our existence that we must accept the reality that seeking greater understanding of its role in our lives is in our best interest. We have much to learn, Dear Friends!

Shall we begin our exploration with another exercise? In participating in this new introspective activity, please give yourself time to thoroughly experience each question that is asked. Don't rush, please! If necessary, address this issue at another time, when you actually have ample time to dedicate to your Self. You deserve the opportunity to fully explore your relationship with inspirational experiences. Let's begin as always with a long restorative, deep breath.

~ B r e a t h e ~

Breathe deeply, Dear Friend.

Know that you are initiating another experience from which you will gain more information about your Self.

Continue your deep breathing until you find a pace and rhythm that is comfortable for you.

Just do what is right for you. This exploration process is for You.

Once again, envision your other companions who are also participating in this exercise and recognize that each of us is doing the work we are intended to do.

We are pursuing more information about who we really are.

When you are ready, Dear Friend, instruct your inner Self to go deeper.

Remember, you are not alone.

Remember to quiet your mind.

Invite the mind to cooperate with you.

Be still as you and your mind adapt to your new surrounds.

And then go deeper.

Welcome the Silence…

Have gratitude for the Silence.

Join with the Silence.

And let the exploration begin.

Remember a time when you experienced being inspired.

How did this experience come about?

Was the inspiration from within or was it received from external sources?

How did you feel at the moment the inspiration registered within you?

As you remember this incident, how does it make you feel now in the present moment?

Over time, have you revisited this inspirational experience? What was the outcome of revisiting the incident?

Did you benefit from revisiting the inspirational experience?

Have you shared your inspirational experiences with others?

Did you benefit from sharing your experience?

Did you notice how the listener was influenced by your story?

Do you feel you are someone who has been blessed with inspirational experiences?

What have you learned from these experiences?
Was there a particular person who inspired you?
Was there a particular place, event, etc., that inspired you?
How did you benefit from the experience?

Do you feel you are someone who has not been blessed with inspirational experiences?

Do any experiences come to mind?
How do you feel about your lack of experiences?
Do you wish to alter that in the future?
If your answer is yes, please continue.
If your answer is no, please continue. It is never too late.

Do you remember times when you inspired another?

How did that individual respond?
What was your response to his or her response?
Did you enjoy the experience?
Would you like to make this a daily practice?
Can you imagine ways that you might inspire others regularly?

Jot your inspirations down for future use.
Do you feel that participating in such an effort would make you feel better about yourself?
Do you feel this type of purposeful action would make you a better person?

◎

For just a moment, imagine the world as a place where no one makes any effort to inspire his or her fellow beings.

Please take a deep breath and recover from that image.

◎

Now imagine a world where everyone consciously, deliberately attempts to inspire others on a daily basis.

Imagine a world where you are the recipient of these efforts on a daily basis.

Imagine a world where you are the presenter of these efforts on a daily basis.

Just imagine what a world like that would be.

◎

Take several more deep breaths.

Express gratitude for what was learned today.

Express gratitude for the good works that you are going to do today and tomorrow and future tomorrows.

Express gratitude that you are evolving into a better person.

In peace be, Dear Friends! As you contemplate what you achieved today, take time to digest your findings and then proceed with a plan. Make a list of ways that you want to consciously and deliberately inspire others. Make another list of people in mind that you want to inspire. And make yet another list of inspirational incidents that you witness as you are out and about living your ordinary day. Training yourself to notice these incidents will brighten your day and change an ordinary day into an extraordinary day. You will also be inspired to participate more fully in these small, but wonderful acts of kindness.

Dear Readers, thank you for participating in this exploration process. As you can see, *Seeking A Better Me!* is not a quick fix. Actually, the book mimics real life. As we pursue new horizons, we experience hurdles, detours, and unexpected opportunities along the way, all of which bring new information for us to consume and digest. Addressing the exercises presented in this book will hopefully assist each of us in our quests to become a better person.

Chapter Nine

*T*he time is now. These four words deserve our attention. What immediately comes to mind when you read these words? Are you excited? Do you feel anticipation rising up within you? Or are you feeling hesitant? Cautious? Is there a bit of dread circling about as well? Or perhaps you are ambivalent! Whatever races through your mind, please try to capture it, because it is important information. Regardless of where you are at this particular moment in time, your reaction to these four words can provide you with more knowledge about your Self.

For instance, it is not uncommon when one reads, sees, hears or experiences something that causes an immediate reaction for that response to be related to a previous event. In situations such as this, the past experience is actually interacting with your current situation.

In our present situation, the prominent four words, *the time is now*, are used purposefully for you to explore and learn more about the workings of your mind. Earlier we discussed the importance of being in charge of your mind rather than allowing it to be in charge of you. In this scenario, you will have an opportunity to gain more information about your leadership role in this fascinating relationship that you have with your mind.

The pronouncement, *the time is now*, seemingly has been overused for ages, yet it is still as purposeful, as it was when it was originally used, and it still continues to generate reactions that are relevant to your evolutionary development. You will have greater understanding of this when you participate in the upcoming exercise.

Dear Readers, as you enter into this exercise, please remember that each of you will have your own unique response to this notable declaration. **The time is now!** Read it again! Hear it within you! What is your immediate reaction to this phrase? What is your unique response?

Please do not be anxious about this exercise. There is nothing to fear. This is simply another opportunity for you to learn more about You.

~ B r e a t h e ~

Sit quietly for a moment.
>Center your Self as you have in previous exercises.
>When you are ready to proceed, engage with the four words of wisdom.
>*The time is now!*
>Just be with this pronouncement.
>Accept whatever you discover without critical commentary.

How is your mind reacting to this declaration?

Is it curious?

Is it open to know more?

Is it suspicious, cautious, negative?

Is it excited, hopeful, anticipatory?

Is it clear and certain?

Is it divided and/or conflicted?

How is your body reacting to this pronouncement?

Do you notice tension or stress anywhere in your body?

If so, where?

Has your breathing pattern changed?

Are you holding your breath?

Are you gasping for breath?

Has your posture changed?

If so, how and where?

How are YOU reacting to these powerful four words?

Are You in charge of your reactions?

Is your mind dominating your reactions?

Are You able to ascertain a clear picture of what is transpiring?

Is there conflict between You and your mind?

Are your reactions consistent with who you are in this moment?

Do your reactions seem to be influenced by the reactions of your mind?

Accept all the information that you have witnessed.
Accept it with gratitude for it will assist you to gain clarity.
Accept the information generated by the mind and compare it with the information that your body is providing you.
Accept the information from both the mind and the body and compare it with whom you believe You are in this moment.

Ponder this abundance of data that has been collected.
Accept all of this information with gratitude.
Thoroughly sort through the information:
Determine what parts of the information are relevant today.
Determine what parts are no longer relevant and can be released.
Determine what parts are in need of improvement.

Celebrate your achievements!
Express gratitude to all who have assisted you along the way.
Express gratitude to Self for all the efforts you are making.
Express gratitude to others who are also striving to become better individuals.
Express gratitude to the Earth for all that she has done on behalf of all her inhabitants.

Breathe deeply and rest…

Dear Readers, thank you for participating in this exercise. Welcome whatever was discovered and congratulate yourself for learning more about who you really are. Perhaps it sounds odd that one must "learn" about oneself, but quite frankly, this is an ongoing, never-ending process. Unfortunately, most of us are so busily distracted with our lives that we don't really know who we are and we mistakenly believe that we are too busy to address such a frivolous notion.

Well, Dear Friends, the time is now! If you are reading this book and/or other books similar to this one then it is highly probable that you are in the process of change. Acknowledging that you are in transition is a recognition that you are indeed changing. In essence, it is your awakening to the reality that it is time for you to discover what is really transpiring. Let's face it, change is always happening, but sadly, it typically happens without our awareness. One can, if so desired, continue to operate from this diminished state of being or one can choose to become actively present and involved in one's transitional process. Hopefully, you will see the merit of the latter option.

Life is ever changing, Dear Friends, so let us take the next bold step together. We could choose a later time, and if it is necessary for some to do so, please know you are still in our hearts and welcome to join with us again at any time of your choosing. However, the question must be asked. If not now, when? Please ponder this!

Whether the decision is now or later, please understand that the transition is already underway and it will continue whether you are consciously present or not. Now is NOT the only opportunity for you to make this decision, but it is the time of relevance. If you choose to delay your involvement in this life-changing event at this time, then turn to your busy calendar and schedule a date when you can actively return to the process. Your participation is important. You are needed!

For those who are ready to make the next step, take a deep breath. Once again, you have chosen to take the lead in your journey. In so doing, you are demonstrating numerous traits that have sustained you throughout this life and others. You have come a very long way gaining strength, confidence, determination, perseverance, faith, and trust, all of which are interacting within you during this self-discovery period. To face the questions that were presented in this latest exercise took courage and strength. With each new question, you pursued your truths and you acquired more information. You persevered while navigating the deepening questions allowing more knowledge to surface. Dear Friend, please be pleased with you. Trust yourself, as do those who are assisting you. This quest to be a better person is not a solo journey. You are accompanied, and these Friends of Old are with you at all times. Even now as you read these words, you are not alone. The previous sentence is more information about your true identity. You are One with all others and you and they are never alone. Hopefully, this ever-expanding truth brings you reassurance and joy.

As you learn more and more about the beautiful Self that you really are, be grateful for this moment in time. Be grateful for You! You created this opportunity and you are the one who did the hard work. You made this possible. There is more good work that remains to be done, but in this moment, just be grateful for all that you have done! You are a remarkable being and you are becoming 'more' every day. You are becoming the 'Better Me!" that you hoped to find.

Chapter Ten

"Once *upon a time, very long ago, there was a planet in a distant galaxy that required assistance. The planet had hosted life and all that accompanies life to those who chose to live their lives from a perspective of peaceful co-existence. This manner of being was most desired throughout all the Greater Existence. Peace reigned on this beautiful planet for ages and all was well until an evolutionary mishap transpired creating massive disruption upon the planet.*

Unfortunately, an element of unknown origins entered into the peaceful environment and rampantly dispersed, causing great changes not seen before. Before the unknown element was introduced into the environment, the inhabitants of the planet lived peaceably with one another. There was no distress among the inhabitants. All life beings respected all other life beings. They lived cooperatively and happily as One.

And then the unknown element, which would come to be known as fear came into being, and life on the planet changed forevermore."

*W*ell, Dear Reader, welcome to the next topic that must be explored. Fear, unfortunately, is an instrumental player in our lives. Whether we know where it originated or not, fear plays a significant role in how we approach life. And as is always the case, each of us has his or her own unique relationship with the topic. Some of you may be wondering if this exercise is appropriate for all situations where fear is involved, and the answer is yet to be known. Hopefully, each of you who is participating in *Seeking A Better Me!* is aware of your own limits. The purpose of these exercises is to gently nudge you forward, but the decision to participate ultimately is up to you. Please have compassion for your Self. If you feel ready to pursue this, then do so at a pace that is right for you. And remember, Dear Reader, you are in charge of your process. If at any time you prefer to stop, then do so.

For those of you who are comfortable with this next challenge, let's begin our next exploration with a deep breath and a commitment to face fear without fear. Obviously, this is easier said than done, but remember, we are not alone. Each of us will gain powerful information about ourselves during this exploration and we will benefit from our efforts. If fear rises up within you and it most likely will, then envision your cohorts (co-hearts!) who are also participating in this exploration. As each of us confronts our fears, fear will diminish from us and from the planet. Isn't that a wonderful image to hold near one's heart? We can do this! You can do this!

~ B r e a t h e ~

Enjoy this time allotted for deep breathing.
> Envision your companions doing the same.
> Accept the reality that you face this next challenge with a Community of Friends.
> As you envision them for support, they do the same with you.
> Have gratitude for this mutual care for one another.

With another deep breath, embrace the idea of being accompanied by Grace on this journey.
> Request that Grace be granted for this important healing experience.
> Request the same for your Community of Friends.
> Accept that Grace is granted.

Another deep breath will assist in preparing you to face your fears.
> Do not hurry through this thoughtful moment.
> Your fears may boldly rush in or
> they may be hesitant to appear.
> Be patient. Be observant.

Notice how your fears are reacting.

If several fears surface at once, select one to be your focus of attention.

Take another deep breath and when you are ready, focus upon the prevalent fear that burdens you.

Remember your purpose is to explore the fear, not to relive it.

Review the known history of this fear, but do not dwell in the misery of it.

How did this fear initially impact you?

How does the fear impact you today?

Analyze the influence that this fear has in your daily life.

Breathe deeply and rest for a moment.

When you are ready to begin again,

face the influence that this dominating fear has upon you daily.

If you do not feel ready to engage in this next step, please do not continue!

Self-care overrides this exercise.

Self-care is appropriate and respected.

Please rejoin us at the end of the exercise.

For those who are continuing, pace yourself as you explore the influence that your lingering fear exerts upon you daily.

Begin by visualizing the fear as originally experienced.

Accept the reality that the fear existed.

Have compassion for you in that initial moment and have compassion for you now in this moment.

Express gratitude for having survived the causative event.

Now, observe the fear as it is today.

Accept the reality that this fearful reaction still exists.

Have deep and persistent compassion for your current circumstances.

Strategize how you wish to diminish the effects of this lingering fear.

Choose to proceed with wisdom as your guide.

An incident that generated fear was experienced.

The fear continues to be intrusive and influential.

You have dominion over your reactions to this fear.

Choose to accept responsibility for dominion over your life.

By accepting responsibility for your own life, you regain your strength and confidence to continue.

When you are strong and confident you can stand face to face with your fears without being fearful.

Choose to view fear from a different perspective.

Fear is powerful if you give your power over to it.

If you look at fear for what it is, a brief moment in time, then you recapture who you really are and you recognize the only power fear has is what you give over to it.

Choose to recognize fear as a momentary moment, and then take a deep breath and reclaim your power.

Fear can no longer frighten us, if we know it for what it truly is: A passing moment that brings forward a message of distress. Once the message is delivered, it no longer has a purpose. Think about this, Dear Friends, fear is a passing moment in time. When you perceive fear in this manner, it loses its power.

Just imagine the positive impact each of us can have on the wellness of the planet if we all reduce the negative energy we produce from our fears. Energy created by fear is extremely toxic to self, others, and Mother Earth. She experiences every emotion that her inhabitants experience. This includes the traumas faced by forests that cannot escape the deadly fires that savage millions of acres across the globe. It includes sea life that cannot hide from the warming oceanic currents and the increasing levels of pollution, and it includes humankind's burdened and depleted energy caused by their unaddressed fears. She bears witness to and experiences every tragic incident that transpires upon her. Mother Earth suffers the consequences of her inhabitants' poor decisions. She needs our help. And we can each play a role in assisting her by reducing and eventually eliminating the negative energy that we produce.

If we would address our fears, one fear at a time, our negative energy that sickens the planet would be significantly reduced. If we are healthier, happier people, the Earth would be released of the burdens of our ill will. Dear Readers, just imagine the ramifications of our efforts to become better people.

Chapter Eleven

"*O*nce upon a time, a Reader was engaging with a book that was bringing forth new information for the Reader to consume. The book guided the Reader to various places, opening the Reader's heart to new truths that were waiting to be known. The Reader faithfully persevered, growing stronger with each page turned until the moment in time came when the Reader needed more than just information.

The Reader, perplexed by the situation pondered what was needed. The answer was not forthcoming, yet the Reader knew that something more was necessary. The Reader paused. The book waited, hoping that the Reader would continue."

Dear Reader, your intuition is keen. You do need something more. That ache inside of you, which keeps repeating that there is more, is speaking the truth. Please do not ignore this inner message. You need something more, because you are more. Do not deny the truth that is rising within you. You are more than you appear to be! How many times do you need to hear this before you will actually accept the reality of your human condition? You are more than you appear to be, and the True You is ready to launch itself. It is time, Dear Reader, for you to accept responsibility for your reason for being. You are here for a reason. This is not a joke. This is your reality. This is your truth.

Breathe, Dear Reader. Just breathe and allow this simple, but incredible message to merge with you. At one level, you have known this truth all your life, and at another level, life was too busy for you to recognize the importance of the message. Regardless of your current life circumstances, please listen with the ears of your heart. The message that you are here for a reason has been presented to you once again.

Please do not walk away from this message. The time is now.

Chapter Twelve

*W*elcome again, Dear Readers. As you might expect, the message received in the previous chapter is the theme of this chapter. I selfishly wish that we could all gather around in a comfy room and discuss our reactions to the ideas that we are more than we appear to be and that we are here for a reason that is beyond merely existing. It would be so fascinating to know how many other people around the globe are also receiving this message. As the last sentence was typed what immediately came to mind was this: Everyone is receiving this message, because we are all here for a reason.

Imagine that, Dear Friends. We are all here for a reason. Wouldn't it be wonderful if we could all awaken to this reality at the same time, so that great changes could transpire more rapidly, if not instantaneously? Perhaps it is time for us to expand our outreach. Throughout this reading experience, we envisioned other Readers participating together in a unified effort to become better people. Maybe it is time for us to think more expansively. From this point forward, let's include everyone in our visionary work. If we are all here for a reason, then let us take our next step by visualizing all of us, every person on the Earth, as the good people we are intended to be.

~Breathe~

Welcome, Dear Friends, to another opportunity for self-discovery.

Breathe deeply and open your heart to possbilities.
The time is now.
Breathe deeper and ponder the possibility
that you are here for a reason.
The time is now.
Slow your breathing to a suitable pace and imagine that this possibility is true.
The time is now.
Visualize yourself in a setting of your choice accepting the reality that you are here for a reason.
The time is now.
Be with this visualization. Embrace the reality, the truth, that you are here for a reason.
The time is now.

~Breathe~

Dear Readers, continue this exercise now with some quality time with your journal. One does not just breeze through such an important realization. Delve deeply within and explore your innermost thoughts and questions before moving on to the next task of the day. This is an important moment in time. As was often repeated...the time is now.

If some of you are feeling overwhelmed and cannot imagine ever being able to identify with the notion that you are here for a reason, then take another deep breath. Rest assured you are not alone. In fact, just for grins, take a moment and visualize your Companions looking about and feeling just as dumbfounded as you feel right now. Dear Readers, you truly are not alone. The message regarding a reason for being has been presented repeatedly for millenia and it is still being delivered to this day. Obviously, you and I, and all of us, are not alone when it comes to addressing this amazing reality. We are here for a reason and the time for accepting this reality is now!

It is time for another exercise, Dear Friends. Please prepare yourself.

~ B r e a t h e ~

Settle your mind, Dear Friend.
Allow the quiet to still your thoughts and your distractions.
Accept the peaceful stillness that engulfs you.
Breathe deeply and enjoy the fullness of the Silence.
Remain in your quiet state as long as is needed.
Embrace these moments of respite.
Find comfort in this Divine state of peace.

When you are ready, open your heart to connection.
Remain still; remain in peace.
Breathe slowly and deeply.
Accept that which is given.

~ B r e a t h e ~

Dear Reader, this contemplative message is one that particularly invites you to access it as needed. It is a gateway to discovering who you really are and what your reason for being is at this point in time.

In truth, we are all here for a reason. Accepting this truth is the first step in recognizing what the reason actually is. Dedication to understanding your reason for being is the next step. Unfortunately, many on the planet Earth have mistakenly come to believe that one's reason for being is elusive and extremely difficult, if not impossible, to discover. That is not the truth! It is a misunderstanding that has disillusioned too many for too long.

This simple, yet powerful exercise opens the door for more information regarding your true identity and your purpose in this lifetime. You, Dear Reader, are a remarkable person who is capable of dedicating the necessary time and effort to secure the information you desire.

This exercise isn't a gimmick. Please read it again, and carefully scrutinize its purpose. Like you, the exercise has a purpose...a reason for being! It is a teaching tool that is purposefully training you to access the Silence for the purpose of discovering the answers that you seek regarding your own purpose for being.

Ponder this, Dear Friend. There is sweet beauty unfolding before you. A very simple exercise that was developed for a reason is presented to an audience of Readers seeking answers regarding their reason for being.

Each of us has a reason for being here at this particular time. Discovering why will facilitate our ability to fulfill in a timely manner the purpose for which we came.

Chapter Thirteen

*O*pen your heart and mind to the reality that your reason for being is the essence of your life. It is the catalyst that awakens you early in the morning and nourishes you throughout the day. It is the source that brings you satisfaction and contentment as you live the life you are intended to experience. When you read or hear the words 'You are here for reason,' please pause and take it seriously.

Dear Readers, as we continue our quest to be better people, these words will be our driving force. "I am here for a reason." The words that appear before you now are the words that have been heard for millennia. This is not new information. It is the information of old coming forward into the present. We have experienced this before in previous lifetimes, and we experience it now, as we are being reminded and primed to accept the role that is intended. As one who found this truth difficult to accept, I shiver as these words come through me. I hope that you will be more open to this message than I was.

Even though I was a person who loved mysterious happenings, I found it curious when I began to hear the message that I was here for a reason. It was odd and I certainly didn't give it any credence…in the beginning.

It never occurred to me that someone like me, who had no inkling of a spiritual life, would have such an unusual experience. At that time, I was very busy with my life as a therapist. In truth, I loved being a therapist. The work was deeply satisfying, and to this day, I remain in awe of my wonderful clients who had the courage to share their stories with me. It was a privilege to witness their sorrows and their progress. I was content with and energized by my work and had no thoughts of changing my vocation.

In retrospect, I now know that my role as a therapist prepared me for the next role. As said, I didn't take the message of purpose seriously in the beginning, but later, after relentless messages were heard, I could no longer deny that something important was happening in my life.

Dear Reader, I hope you will be a faster learner than me. When I first heard, 'You're here for a reason," I thought it was a joke, and quickly turned about to see who the prankster was. You will not be surprised when I admit that there was no one else in the room with me. At least no one that was visible. I look back on that time now with a smile on my face. I was so naïve, so unaware.

The message of old is indeed a wakeup call. I urge you to pay attention when you begin receiving this message. You can ignore it, as I did, but that just delays the process. Over time, I came to realize that the message was actually a gift. Initially, it certainly did not seem so. It was just something curious that was happening that I chose to believe did not require my attention. Then, because I wouldn't give the message the attention it deserved, the frequency of the repeated message increased to the point that it was an annoyance. Let me be honest about this. The messenger didn't have another choice! I was so certain that my life was as it should be, that I was resistant to any other possibility.

Eventually, my stubborn nature quieted and my heart finally opened to the message. I am so grateful that the presenters of the message persisted. He/she/they never gave up! Thank you, thank you, thank you!

Life profoundly changed thereafter, and it continues to do so on a daily basis. That's what life does. And now, after all those years of listening to clients, I find myself in another vocation where I am still a listener. Who knew that all those wonderful people, who shared their lives with me, were actually preparing me for another type of listening? Gratitude abounds!

I'm still a Listener, but now I listen to the Silence. Who knew the Silence had so much to say?

Dear Reader, thank you for listening to my story. I hope you will respond to the message of purpose more quickly than me. It truly is a gift.

Chapter Fourteen

"Once upon a time, there was a time when time did not matter. It was a time of great peace. It was a time when time did not dictate how one experienced his or her time. Time was not noticed during this period because time was timeless and how one spent the timeless time was of no matter to anyone. Those were remarkable times."

Dear Reader, in one's journey to become the better person that you desire to be, you must have an encounter with time, and now is the time to do so.

If the idea of discussing time gives you the shivers, then take a deep breath. Time is not the enemy. Although there are times when time seems to be working against you, in actuality, time is not the issue. Time comes and time goes, but it has no intentions other than to be a defining feature of time. So, your relationship with time that developed over time is actually a one-sided perspective. While you were concerned about time, time did what time does. Time merely existed.

Let us begin our exploration of time with an existential truth about time. The present is the moment of relevance. What has transpired in the past is of the past and what will unfold in the future is yet to be, and while one may ponder about these times that are not of the present, it is unwise to dwell in these times that distract you from the relevant moment before you.

Often incidents from past experiences play significant roles in our present lives and it can be extremely helpful to explore those important scenarios in order to more fully understand who we are in the moment. With greater understanding, each of us can ascertain if we are the person we truly want to be. Dear Reader, regard this process as an opportunity of time: time to truthfully and honestly observe who you are. Time to celebrate your positive attributes, and time to lovingly and compassionately face the parts of you that need improving. Time to live life consciously while being aware of your impact upon others. Time to fulfill the goal of becoming the better person that you desire to be.

Time is available, Dear Reader, so let's engage with another exercise.

~ B r e a t h e ~

Prepare yourself by settling into a state of relaxation.
Take your deep breaths.
Find the pace and rhythm that is right for you.
Sink deeper into the state of relaxation that will open your heart to acceptance.
Breathe deeply again.
Adapt to the possibility of acceptance.
Trust yourself.

You are capable of accepting yourself.
You are capable of accepting others.
You are capable of being an accepting person.
Breathe this reality in.

As your heart opens, focus upon You.
Recall memories/incidents from the past that require your attention.

As each comes to mind, remember it with gentle care.

Hold to your heart that which is cherished.
Release whatever is no longer needed.
Make a note of that which needs additional contemplation.
Accept who you were.
Breathe this reality in.
Continue with the next segment of your exploration when you are able to do so.
Self-care is critical in this delicate introspective work.

Review moments/incidents in the present that require your attention.

As each comes to mind, remember it with gentle care.

Hold to your heart that which is cherished and gain comfort from these positive experiences.
Revel in these moments; allow them to empower you.

Give yourself permission to cast aside whatever
can be purged at this point.
    Trust yourself.
    Accept that you are empowered to make this
    decision.
    Breathe this reality in.
Carefully approach current issues.
    Address issues that can be managed now with
    honesty, courage, and integrity.
    Assess your progress and make a note of issues
    that need additional consideration.
    Accept who you are.
Accept who you are becoming.

Breathe deeply again and reflect upon what was
accomplished by participating in this exercise.
    Make notes about your reflections: These findings
    will be beneficial in the days ahead.
Express gratitude for what has been achieved.
    Create a list of your current appreciations for
    those moments when you forget how abundant
    your blessings are.
Take another deep breath and accept how fortunate
you are.
    Accept who you are now in this moment.
        Breathe this reality in.
    Accept who you are becoming.
        Breathe this truth in.
    Have confidence in who you are.
        Gain strength from the growth you are witnessing.

Inhale deeply as you enter another opportunity for improvement.

Face the issues that still require your attention.

Do this at a pace that is right for you.

Take one issue at a time, resting when needed, and continuing when you are ready to proceed.

This is not a race.

Self-care is essential.

Once again, make notes about your reflections regarding each issue.

These reminders keep you on track, especially when breaks are taken between issues.

Remember speed is not the issue.

Quality time is necessary for healing to occur.

Transformational issues are not stagnant; they are an ongoing process that requires patience, perseverance, and tender self- care.

Trust yourself! You are capable of engaging with and surviving these challenges.

You are more than you appear to be.

You are becoming the one you are intended to be:

Ever growing,

Ever changing,

Ever expanding,

Ever becoming.

Breathe this reality in, Dear Friend.

You are who you are intended to be.

~ B r e a t h e ~

Dear Friend, I am most grateful for your participation in this chapter. Although this is not easy work, it is essential for your personal growth. I hope you are singing your praises at this significant moment in time. By participating in this process, you are personally, deliberately accelerating your transformational process. Yay! Thank you for your efforts!

As you applaud yourself at this time, also applaud all the other participants who are also purposefully propelling their developmental process forward. Together, you are changing the course of history, and in so doing, you are healing Self, the Earth, and the future of humanity. What you are doing is important! Hold this truth near to your heart as you continue moving forward.

Chapter Fifteen

"***O****nce upon a time, Dear Friend of Mine, when you came into existence, time mattered. Yes, the day that you appeared, time mattered because you, Dear Child of Mine were exquisite in every way, and All who were already in existence, were overwhelmed with your presence. Imagine this truth, Dear Friend, and you will finally have a glimpse of who you really are. Since the beginning of your existence, you have been loved, adored, and cherished by all others in existence. This is true for you and for every other in existence as well. So deeply appreciated are you that mere words cannot possibly express the fullness of your presence to all of your companions in existence. Simply stated, you are more than you appear to be. You matter to all others with whom you share this remarkable existence.*"

Dear Reader, the previous paragraph is presented in italics to clarify its importance. Read each word as if it were specifically written for you, because it is! It is a gift intended for You! Please accept it.

Let's engage in another exercise.

~ B r e a t h e ~

Please, take a moment to settle yourself, Dear Friend.
A few deep breaths will take you to that place of
peaceful serenity.
When you reach that sense of stillness, please
read the italicized paragraph again.
Read it slowly…
as if you were reading it to someone
whom you desire to fully understand, and
accept the truth
that is revealed in the message.
See the words before you…
Gently touch the words with your preferred
finger as you read them aloud or silently…
Hear the words…
Listen with the ears of your heart…
Feel each breath as you take the message in…
Feel the energy that is attached to each word…
Grasp the emotion that engulfs the message.
Accept the message as it is given…
Embrace the message…
Accept it as your own…
You are more than you appear to be!
And you are loved, adored, and cherished!
Accept this truth, for it is your truth!

~ B r e a t h e ~

Accept this truth, for it is your truth! These are powerful
words that demand our attention. Many of us have already

experienced conversations with the Inner Voice. The messages of wisdom and support that come forward are often difficult to accept because they are so tender...so beautiful. In truth, the messages are so beyond our scope of imagination that we cannot readily believe that these encounters are real, or even begin to fathom that the messages presented are actually intended for one's Self.

Dear Reader, this message is real, but it will not be successfully delivered if the recipient, you, refuses to accept it. Wouldn't that be sad for all of us? Why is it that we can see the best in others, but cannot do the same for ourselves? What a waste! Why attempt to seek a 'Better Me' if we are unwilling to accept the truth about one's Self?

We have a challenge that must be faced. Let's choose to do it together! Please read the italicized message again and this time imagine all your companions who are also participating in *Seeking A Better Me!'* As you envision their efforts in this process, wish them well. Applaud their successes and have compassion for their hurdles. Cheer them on! Remind them that they are loved, adored, and cherished. Remind them that they are more than they appear to be. Do this loving gesture on their behalf and ask them to accept what you are saying to them. Ask them to believe the truth that you are telling them. Do this, Dear Reader. Please do this for your companions. Ask them to receive and accept the gift that you are offering them.

And now, you must do the same. You must willingly receive and accept the gift that is being offered to you.

Breathe this in, Dear Readers. Just imagine the difference this act of generosity can have if we just allow ourselves to accept the reality that we are loved, adored, and cherished. Just imagine if we accept that we are more than we appear to be. Just imagine if Everyone begins to accept Everyone equally. What a transformation that would be!

Chapter Sixteen

*O*nce again we face a new chapter with a new theme. Brace yourselves, Dear Readers, for this topic is one that may be difficult. Not to worry though, you are ready for this challenge. Just prepare yourself with a deep breath and envision your companions doing the same. Together, we will face this issue that burdens many of us. For those of you who are not aware of this complicated issue, please participate in the exercise anyway. It is an opportunity for you to learn more about a significant human trait that is extremely damaging to humankind's development.

The reason this issue is so complicated is that most people are completely unaware that they are afflicted with the problem. In fact, the afflicted tend to be steadfast in their denial of the idea.

So here we are. We are about to address a problem that most of us need to deal with, while at the same time, most of us are clueless that we suffer from the issue. This is a challenge that must be faced and it is best done in unity with our companions.

Let us begin this important exercise with a deep, satisfying breath and the image of all of us standing hand-in-hand offering support and assistance to one another.

~ B r e a t h e ~

See your companions standing in unity and sharing good wishes with one another.

> Feel the safety and camaraderie of their presence and feel the joy of offering the same to them.
>
> Open your heart to possibilities, as you choose to become a better person by addressing the unfolding issue.

Allow a sense of peace to engulf you.

> Breathe this grace-filled entity in and allow the wonderful presence of peace to touch every cell within you.
>
> As you exhale, direct the peaceful particles to surround you, creating a cycle of breathing in and out that maintains and sustains the peaceful state.

From this peaceful state, we are now ready to proceed with the task at hand.

> With the next deep breath, give yourself permission to consider the possibility that you are a person of judgment.
>
> Simply consider the possibility.

Avoid entering a state of denial.

Avoid the temptation of feeling insulted.

Avoid the idea of being judged.

Avoid feeling righteously indignant.

Simply consider the possibility.

Open your heart to the possibility that you experience moments of judgment towards self and others.

Applaud yourself for having the courage to explore this possibility.

Reassure yourself that you are a person of goodness who is capable of facing this possibility.

Accept the reality that this possibility is worth your time and energy to explore.

Take another deep breath and rejuvenate your peaceful state.

Once again allow the grace-filled energy of peace to engulf and embrace you.

Breathe comfortably at a pace that is right for you.

Attend you with the tender care that you deserve.

Applaud yourself for taking another step towards being the better person that you are seeking to be.

~ B r e a t h e ~

Let's pause for a moment, Dear Readers. As you can see, we are entering into a topic that truly is complicated and uncomfortable. Unfortunately, this topic typically results in heated reactions, which are unpleasant for all involved. Nevertheless, these reactions demonstrate how important it is for us to gather more information about our judging nature.

This inclination to judge self and others is prevalent among all cultures and across all lands. We cannot continue turning our eyes away from the truth that our judging ways are extremely harmful to all of us. Anyone who has experienced the judging nature of another can attest to that reality. And anyone who does not recognize this as a serious problem needs to open his or her eyes to the reality of what is transpiring around us.

In order to become the better person we are each seeking to become, we must address this issue. We must do so with kindness and compassion. There is no place for critical commentary or judging behavior when we are exploring our personal acts of "Self and Other" judgment. Yes, Dear Friends, we must explore ourselves first and we must do so with tender care. We must be truthful and honest about our self-judgment and about our judgment of others. We must listen carefully to the words we speak, to the thoughts we think, and we must bear witness to our actions. The goal is to become informed about our behaviors without shaming or punishing ourselves in the process.

It is highly likely that many of us will be surprised by what we discover, because we do not believe that we are judgmental. Thus, we are blind to our own behaviors.

This exploratory process is necessary and will assist us in discerning how unkind and judging we are towards others and ourselves. Unfortunately, it is also likely that we will momentarily revert to our old habits when we encounter our old behaviors that were previously denied and/or ignored. Dear Readers, just take a deep breath and please be exceptionally good to yourselves during this exploration. Seek the information that you need to know to improve yourself and bear its discomfort. Then, braced by your preparatory efforts, make the necessary changes to extricate yourself from the old ways of being. We are all capable of changing. We can do this. And when we do, others will change as well.

Judging is an infectious behavior. Picture it as a highly contagious disease spreading rapidly around the globe. The longer it goes untreated, the more problematic it becomes. It flares at times, resulting in conflicts and wars and then momentarily recedes while more unkindness, meanness, and hatred builds until it is ready to flare again. Unstable, yet persistent, the cycle seems to be ongoing, never-ending. It is time to test that misguided belief. It is time to squelch the negativity of this behavior with goodness. By becoming the better people we are intended to be, we can put a stop to the cruelty that plagues our planet. This problem cannot be corrected with aggression. We know that doesn't solve the issue. Another method must be found. One that eliminates unkindness with kindness, one that replaces cruelty with humane care and dignity, and one that hallows humanity rather than heralding inhumanity.

It requires courage to stand up to judging behavior, but it can be done. And we will begin by confronting our own judging nature first. Trust yourself, Dear Friend. You can encounter the judging aspect in yourself and you can assist that part of you to become a better person. As you are doing your work, so too will all the other Readers who are pursuing this new way of being. Trust yourself, and trust your companions. Together, a new way of being is possible.

Dear Readers, applaud yourself and your companions for continuing. This project of self-improvement is indeed demanding, but worth the effort. Every action that you take on your behalf improves your future and the future of everyone around you. Just as humankind's negativity spreads around the globe, so too will these positive improvements, and positive energy is far more powerful than negative energy. As good will becomes the predominant nature of the people of Earth, great changes will occur across the planet. Strife among families, communities, and nations will become a rarity. Outrageous behaviors will no longer be accepted as the norm. Instead, such rare incidents will be noted as an issue that is in need of compassionate care.

If you find this difficult to believe, just know that you are in good company. We have grown so accustomed to the prevalence of ill will in our society that we accept it as a given and we cannot imagine life without it. We erroneously presume that ill will is irreversible.

Dear Readers, we are more than we appear to be. And it is time that we accept a truth that has been forgotten. We, meaning every person on this planet, are more than we presently seem to be. We are more than our ill will. We are not intended to be people of anger, hatred, and violence. This is not who we are intended to be, and we have the power to change this tragedy. Each of us has the power to change. We do not have to accept the old way of being.

Take a deep breath, Dear Readers. Within each of us is an opportunity for improvement. We are given opportunities every day to make choices. Some of you who are in extremely difficult situations will rightly disagree with this statement. And because of your difficulties, it is essential that the rest of us rise to the occasion. As we face the challenges to improve ourselves, particularly in the arena of judgment, we must realize that our growth will come incrementally, and not all of us will have the pleasure or the luxury of changing as rapidly as those who have less complicated situations.

Each of us is obliged to do the best she or he can in the moment, and while we applaud our own achievements, let us not forget those whose circumstances are much more difficult than our own. This self-development project is for the good of all. It is not intended to ignite competition. Instead it will hopefully spark humanity's good will. The positive changes that are made daily will improve the energy of humankind, which in turn will improve the positive energy of our Dear Earth. These changes will matter, and eventually everyone will be touched by the changes.

Dear Reader, please pause for a moment. You have just received an enormous amount of information. This wasn't just a pep talk intended to jump-start your transformational process. In truth, it was an appeal for help. You are needed! Each of us is needed! We each have a role to play.

As you well know, humans are not a species that appreciate being told what to do, even when the truth is being spoken. An exceptional example of this is the issue of the Earth's declining health. Rather than being curious and seriously concerned about this catastrophic situation, we have witnessed years of division, disgruntlement, and delays. Not only have the planet's health issues been ignored, but so too has the future of humankind. This is a truth that can no longer be denied; yet there are those who insist upon continuing their inconceivable disregard for the planet. Needless to say, their motives are suspect. Evidence of the environmental crisis is boundless. The instigators and distributors of misinformation clearly have intentions that are not in alignment with the health of the Earth. Their misguided antics perpetuate more confusion and delays, none of which serves the future of humankind.

Unfortunately, our irrational behaviors are a major factor in the Earth's decline. Our mistreatment of each other and ourselves severely harms the planet. If this truth doesn't make sense to you, then please take a moment to give it serious consideration. When you witness someone shaming, humiliating, or brutally harming another, how does that make you feel? I'm not referring to something you see on television or in the movies, although those experiences are also evidence of the problem. Please think of a time when you have witnessed or been the recipient of an act of senseless meanness. How did that make you feel? Let yourself feel that incident again, now in the present. And then, you will understand the impact these acts of unkindness are having on the Earth. Wherever these abusive incidents occur around the globe, Mother Earth is there, witnessing and feeling the horror of our cruel behaviors. She is always present! She cannot escape our inhumanity. Then, take another step in understanding the impact of our negative manners by imagining what it is like when bombs are exploded upon her or poisonous products are buried within her or dumped into her oceans. She is a Life Being and she feels everything that transpires upon her. She is profoundly impacted by our behavior. The Earth deserves better.

Dear Readers, there are many reasons why we should improve ourselves.

In essence, it's just the right thing to do. When we stop a moment and truly think about the impact we have on others, we then realize that our presence in the world truly matters. How we behave matters! How we treat others matters! Our presence matters! Why not choose to live life in a way that positively impacts the world? One small change can make a difference.

Seeking A Better Me! invites us to do that and more. Just remember that each of us can improve ourselves and the more we do so, the more we personally benefit, as do those around us. The appeal made in this chapter is truly asking us to participate in the quest to be a better person. Let's do it together now by experiencing another exercise.

~ B r e a t h e ~

Take the deep breath that will enable you to rise to the occasion of becoming the better person you strive to be.

Enjoy this ritual of self-care for as long as you need.

You are in charge of your journey.

Allow the breath to lead your exploration.

When you are ready, open your heart to the inner work that awaits you.

With your next deep breath, express gratitude for this opportunity of expansion.

Thank yourself for participating in this wondrous process of growth.

Thank your companions around the world who also take this next step of self-improvement.

Thank those from the past who come to mind, who have assisted you along the journey, even if their roles were complicated and challenging.

Thank those of the present who inspire opportunities for change, whether their roles have been supportive or challenging.

Be grateful that you are both physically and mentally in a place where you can initiate this process.

Be grateful that your heart has opened to the possibility of making positive changes.

Be grateful that you are here now, consciously present and able to make the changes that you discern are necessary for the future.

Breathe in the fullness of your gratefulness and allow this cleansing and empowering energy to touch every cell within you.

Emboldened by this expansive energy just created, take the next step towards becoming the person you desire to be.

As with all new adventures into the precious Self that you are, it is wise to prepare with several, deep refreshing breaths.

Once again, take care of your process: set your own pace, and continue in a way that is right for you.

When ready, inhale deeply, and invite a situation of interest to surface for review.

Welcome the situation with an open heart, remembering that you are in command of this encounter.

With gratitude and compassion in your heart, honestly review your role in the situation.

Refrain from negative remarks or thoughts: this is an opportunity to change old habits.

With kindness, acknowledge your behaviors whether they are positive or negative.

Review your positive behaviors and determine ways of improving them.

Bear witness to any negative behaviors noticed and strategize how to change these patterns.

Recognize that some behaviors are more resistant to change than others, and remember your resolve to change.

Practice new ways of verbalizing your thoughts and preferences that are founded in kindness and goodness.

Practice new ways of behaving that facilitate connection rather than dissension.

Practice a new way of listening: listen with your heart rather than your ears.

Accept what you are witnessing with compassion.

Applaud that you recognize problem areas.

Applaud that you are making improvements.

Graciously accept that there are more improvements to be made.

Express your appreciation to everyone who participated in the exercise.

Express your appreciation to Self for all that you have done to improve yourself.

~ B r e a t h e ~

Before proceeding with the remainder of this exercise, let us rest for a moment. As each of you well know, the inward journey can be taxing and exhilarating simultaneously. During these times of great transition, it is essential that one proceeds with gentle care. You decide when it is best for you to continue and you decide when it is best to rest.

Do not worry about taking breaks. This work is intense and there are times when you need to stop and focus upon other matters. Trust yourself! You will be able to return to the exercise and re-establish your rhythm. Our goal of becoming a better person is an ongoing process. We will be refining ourselves throughout our lifetime. Your commitment to this process is already in progress and it will continue as long as you desire to be more than you presently are. Every day is an opportunity to be a better 'You!'

In our next exercise, we will specifically focus our attention upon our judging tendencies towards others. If the idea makes you want to go attend to some other task, don't worry about it. Once again, realize that you are in good company. Let's be honest here! Who really wants to explore their own ill will? After all, that's what judgment really is. Many of us are blind to our unkindness. We don't listen to the tone in our voice, nor do we think that we are being awful, when in fact, we really are being hurtful and mean to another person. This topic is important, because many of us truly don't know how offensive we can be. Unless someone challenges us about our behavior, we remain clueless, and because of our lack of awareness, we continue to be an unpleasant person spreading negativity to everyone near us. Having acknowledged this does not mean that we are not responsible for our actions. We are responsible for how we affect others and we should hold ourselves accountable. We have an obligation to pay attention! We cannot expect the people that we have wounded to apprise us of our meanness.

We must pay attention and witness the impact we have on others.

Dear Friends, the assertion that most of us are not aware of our offending ways is not proven by statistics; however, you will be astounded when this topic is discussed how surprised individuals are that they have judging behaviors that are harming others.

It is also important for us to make note that there are individuals who purposefully, deliberately, and intentionally participate in ill will. While everyone is invited to seek a better path, there are some who will choose not to do so. Although this is unfortunate, the opportunity to change will always be available to them. In the meantime, those who seek to improve their skills in loving kindness and good will are invited to continue expanding their positive energy for the sake of others, the planet, the universe, and self. All will benefit from seeking to be a better person. With hopeful hearts and optimistic minds, let's proceed with the next exercise.

~Breathe~

Yes, Dear Reader, let's begin with another refreshing, long breath. Please remember that you are in charge of your process. Address this exercise in a manner that is congruent with who you are at this moment in time. If you prefer to start at another time, do so. Trust yourself. Everyone participating in these exercises has other obligations that must be attended. Trust your companions to return to this important work when it is convenient. Likewise, they will trust you as well. Becoming a better person is a daily experience; it must be woven into the tapestry of your current life. So once again, those who are ready, let's take the next breath together.

◎

As you sink deeply into your peaceful state, express appreciation for the luxury of participating in this self-care experience.

Express gratitude for your companions far and near.

Hold these new friends in your heart as you move deeper into the silence.

Breathe at a pace that serves you.

Open yourself to new possibilities.

◎

When you are ready to take the step into exploring the negative aspects of your judging nature, do so with compassion, gentle care, and optimism.

With courage and humility select an incident from your life experiences, which demonstrates your judging inclinations.

Review the incident as best you can.

Assess your role in the incident.

What were the circumstances that caused you to overtly or covertly respond negatively?

Was your response logical or illogical?

Was it founded in truth or supposition?

Was it necessary? Did your action improve the situation?

Assess your impact on the other person.

>Do you have any idea how you affected the other person?

>Did you see a reaction?

>Was it positive or negative?

>Was there an improvement in the other person's behavior?

>Did your action harm the other person?

Assess your impact on you?

>How did you feel at the time of the incident?

>How do you feel now after reviewing your behavior?

>What have you learned from this review of the incident?

In retrospect, would you alter what transpired?

>If so, how?

Rest now, please.

>Later, when it is convenient for you, consider having a session with your journal. Wisdom often surfaces through this age-old method of cleansing one's heart and soul.

~ B r e a t h e ~

Thank you, Dear Friends, for accepting the challenge of facing your judging behaviors. Not only have these exercises opened our hearts to a part of ourselves that needs attention, reflection, and refinement, they have also assisted us in recognizing that we are capable of change. Some of us may be feeling very raw and exposed at the moment, and if that is your situation, then please take a good rest. You've expended a great deal of energy. Take time to regain your strength.

What was achieved today is just the beginning. Praise yourself for what you have done and remember: you are a person of goodness who is becoming more and more grace-filled every day.

Rest now, Dear Friend. In peace be.

Chapter Seventeen

*I*n this chapter, we will address another aspect of our human nature that is a challenge for our species. Although we are a remarkable species with infinite potential, we also are a species impaired by many misunderstandings regarding our station in the world. One would presume that a species with unlimited potential would be in alignment with the needs of the planet upon which they live; however, this is not the case. Not only are we unable to live peaceably among our own species, but we also are disinterested in and reckless towards other species that also inhabit the planet.

Why this callous, cold-hearted attitude exists demands our attention. Similar to our other judgmental ways, we once again exhibit lack of awareness and empathy for those around us. It is true that there are exceptions to this statement. There are those who adore the Earth and treat her with great care and there are others who actually are curious and concerned about their fellow beings. If only there were more of these caring, loving people. If that were true our planet would be much healthier, and we humans would be safer and much more pleasant to coexist with.

Acknowledging the truth that our species is the primary factor in Earth's problems is a step in the right direction.

Until we accept this reality, we will continue our old ways of arrogance misled by our own pride and sense of entitlement. It's a choice that our species has to make. We can choose to continue our current misguided ways that are leading us down a path that will end in great tragedy, or we can just admit the truth. Our present behaviors are not indicative of a species with great potential.

How much longer is it going to take for us to accept that killing one another is insane. It is not normal behavior! Nor is defiling the planet upon which we live. A species that is as gifted as ours should be able to recognize that we are behaving erratically. We are not functioning in a manner that sustains our species or those around us. We are not well. Our behavior is evidence of that.

What will it take for humankind to accept that we need to alter our present behaviors? We need to do it for ourselves, for our descendants, for the well being of the future. As this book is being received, I wonder if the fears of the elders of today are also held by the youth of today, and part of me says, please spare them from this fear. But another part of me does not want them to move forward in ignorance and naiveté. Information about the Earth's decline has been known and made available for decades, and still, we turn our eyes away from the truth. The young of today cannot be held responsible for the wrongs that we have done. This is our burden to address. We are the ones who have to step up and acknowledge what is really going on.

We cannot pretend that we do not play a role in the issues that are unfolding around the globe. This is not to say that every one of us is a perpetrator of ill will, but we are witnesses of it. We know it exists and each of us must decide how we personally can improve ourselves, which will thereby improve the global situation. Self-improvement comes in many packages. A simple smile can change another's day. A helping hand is always needed. The list of opportunities for healing humanity is endless. The point is we must accept that we have behaviors that need improvement and each of us must hold ourselves accountable for taking action.

The idea of being accountable is an issue that also demands attention. When we begin assessing our present behavior, there will be an inclination to switch our focus to another's behavior. Let's face it. It is much easier to recognize judgmental behavior in another than it is to accept it in oneself. So when we find that we are pointing fingers at someone else rather than ourselves, we must recognize what we are doing and refocus upon self. The goal is to assess self and improve self. Assessing someone else's behavior is a distraction from evaluating one's own behavior. It's an avoidance tactic.

Our resistance to accepting our own judging nature is strong. We just do not want to believe this about ourselves. Dear Readers, please open your heart to this human frailty. We are human and we are susceptible to this unfortunate behavior. However, please remember that we are a species with great potential, and we can certainly overcome this unpleasant and harmful human trait. Take comfort in knowing that you are not alone in this self-improvement project and simply commit to holding yourself accountable. If each of us makes a commitment to address this unacceptable characteristic within us, significant change will follow.

Before we engage with the next exercise, let's remember several important points of our discussion regarding this problematic issue. First and foremost, each of us is and remains a person of goodness. Just because we struggle with a potentially harmful issue that is embarrassing for us to acknowledge does not mean that we cannot overcome the problem. We are all capable of change, and now that we are sufficiently aware of the side effects of our judging nature, we can put an end to this heartless behavior.

Once again, let us remember that we enter into this next exercise in the company of many others who also are determined to eradicate these unkind episodes from our way of being. Dear Ones, take your deep breaths with a smile on your face. You are on the path of profoundly changing your future.

~Breathe~

With each deep breath, accept that you are a person of goodness.
Remember a moment when you participated in an act of kindness.
When you shared a sweet greeting with another.
When you offered words of consolation.
When you encouraged, inspired, cheered, or simply smiled at someone.

When you opened the door for someone, or helped an elder with a task that was no longer easy for him/her to manage.
Make a list of times when you acted kindly towards another and hold this list in your heart.
Remember the kindnesses that you have offered others.

◎

Take a moment to express your appreciation for the memories of your actions of good will.
Each memory is a demonstration of your kindness flowing out to others.
Cling to these memories for they will strengthen your awareness of the goodness that resides within and the abilities that you have to share this exceptional part of you.
The better person that you seek already resides within.
Express your gratitude for who you are and who you are yet to be.

◎

Take a deep breath as you prepare to address your resistance to your judging nature.
Select an incident in which you thought, spoke or acted unkindly to another.
Review your behavior with honesty and an open heart.
Assess your actions and reactions without self-punishing remarks.

This is an opportunity to learn more about you.
It is not an opportunity for scolding, shaming, or diminishment.
Notice your reactions to your behavior.
Do you feel defensive?
Do you feel resistant?
Do you feel embarrassed or ashamed?
Do you feel the need to justify your behavior?
Are you able to simply accept the reality of your behavior?
Can you accept your disappointment in your behavior?
Can you express your sadness and regrets to yourself?
Can you analyze your behavior and make plans for change?
Can you forgive yourself for your human flaws?
Can you trust yourself to alter the behaviors that need improvement and move beyond the behaviors that impair your potential to be a better you?

Praise the New You that you are becoming.
Every day move forward with determination to be a better person.
Every day observe your behaviors and assess if you are on the right path to becoming the You that you desire to be.

Every day accept what you observe honestly and truthfully.

Praise yourself for the goodness that is emanating from you.

Correct the issues that demand more attention.

Repeat these tasks every day for all eternity.

Dear Readers, thank you for participating in this exercise. As you can see self-improvement is a life long commitment that truly is an essential element of our lives. Obviously, there will be times when we are not at our best, and hopefully some day, those times will be rare. But in the meantime, our commitment to become a better person will be attained if we remain consciously aware of our daily behaviors. If we pay attention, we will witness when we are behaving appropriately, and we will also recognize when we are out of alignment with our better self. As we continue to practice becoming a better person, we will instantly know when our behavior is not meeting our preferred standards, and we will choose to quickly address the situation. It's just that simple. Once one has established a way of being that is satisfying, joyful, meaningful, and filled with good will, one is not inclined to settle for anything less. The habit of becoming a better person creates a consistently better person. As you practice being who you desire to be, you become the better person you desire to be.

Chapter Eighteen

*I*n peace be, Dear Reader. We now embark upon another chapter and another topic that hopefully will inspire each of us to continue our efforts towards becoming a better person. Perhaps some of you are wondering if this process will ever come to an end. The answer to that deliberation is easy. We are Life Beings innately driven by the desire to evolve. We grow, we pause, we rest, and we begin again. Sometimes we take giant leaps while other times, our steps are glacial and seem non-existent. Regardless of the progress being made at any time, whether it is noticeable or not, rest assured you are indeed in the process of becoming more than you were before. Even when we are in periods that seem to be stagnant, we are still evolving. Seldom do we recognize this in the moment, but often in hindsight the importance of our so-called slow periods become apparent.

Those of you who are participating in this reading project are definitely in transition. Congratulate yourself and your reading companions for the achievements made thus far. Changes are happening. Applaud your forward motion and continue to monitor the situations that are not progressing as rapidly as you had anticipated. Simply observe with curiosity. This is an approach that is strategically wise because it allows for discernment, which leads to implementation of new ways of continuing and sustaining improvements. Please remember to be alert to any old negative habits that may surface during these periods. As you well know condescending comments and thoughts are not helpful and should be avoided. In truth, they are a waste of time and energy that should be released as quickly as possible.

Now, Dear Reader, a conversation regarding the future is necessary. We will begin by speaking of the present. Today is the day that sets the stage for the rest of this life experience.

How you proceed matters!
How you live your life matters!

Do these heartfelt statements mean that there is an exact path that you are intended to follow? It's possible. Anything is possible, which you will discover as you continue your quest to be a better person. However, rarely does one's path follow a direct line. The universe is far too spirited and expansive to provide such a limited evolutionary experience.

Perhaps, Dear Reader, these profound statements are a gentle reminder prompting you to remember that your life is significant in its own unique way. To fully engage with and understand your life's purpose, you must be consciously present as it unfolds. Only then will you recognize what you are to do when various options, hints and nudges surface along your path of self-discovery.

Just in case you haven't noticed it, you are now in this moment on the brink of such a position. You are traveling along a path that is presenting you with an opportunity to think about how you will proceed forward from this point in time.

Together, let us all take the next step together. Once again, envision your companions who have joined with you throughout this reading experience. Enjoy the smiles that are being shared and the silent expressions of gratitude that are circling the globe. So fortunate have we been to share this experience with one another. The time has come for each of us to focus our attention upon creating a plan for the future. Seeking to be a better person, a Better Me, does not end with the completion of this book. Dear Friends, each of us is a work-in-progress!

The more we practice being the better person that we desire to be, the more we will actualize that person. And without doubt, as we make strides toward this sought-after better state of being, new challenges and new awareness will come along that demand us to review ourselves over and over again. Our evolutionary process requires constant attention…always seeking, always discovering, always pondering, always evolving.

But now, let us return to the present moment that demands our attention. Soon your frequent encounters with this book will come to a close; however, the practice developed during this adventure must continue. Obviously, the book will be available when necessary, but the time to proceed without it is upon you. The skills are within you.

The desire is within you. Now, the plan that will assist you from this point forward awaits your attention.

Let us begin with the breath that sustains us and propels us to places of serenity and knowingness.

~ B r e a t h e ~

Sit quietly.
Allow your breath to take you inward.
Invite all distractions to relocate to a preferred holding area where they can be addressed later.
Seek comfort in the silence.

Open your heart to growth, expansion, and new beginnings.
Settle deeply within the silence.
Rest there, as the silence attends you…
    Accept the revitalized energy that is offered.
    Accept the courage that is fortified.
    Accept the wisdom that is offered.
    Accept the truths that are shared.
Embody all that has been given.

With the assistance of the silence, focus your attention upon creating a plan for maintaining your practice in the future.
    Review your recent achievements.
        Record these achievements so that they are easily accessible, if needed.

These notes are a history of your forward motion.

They are a reminder of where you have been and how far you have come.

Review issues that interfered with your progress.

Assess how the issues were managed.

Offer suggestions for future management.

Strategize ways of maintaining and expanding your progress.

Resist retreating to old behaviors that interfere with or delay forward motion.

Applaud your good work.

Rest briefly and express your appreciation for all that has been achieved and noted.

Once again, with the assistance of the silence, focus your attention upon creating a maintenance plan for your future practice.

Strategize ideas for continuing your practice.

Review your recent experiences.

Assess what worked well for you.

Determine changes that will be beneficial

Devise a new schedule that is in alignment with the changes that are being made.

Strategize ideas for expanding your practice.

Make a list of thoughts, ideas, dreams that are related to becoming a better person.

Ponder how you will put these ideas into action.

How will you proceed?

When will you initiate the first idea?

Devise a plan for reviewing and assessing each
idea once initiated.

Strategize options for future moments when your
practice wanes.

Refrain from any negative commentary about the
situation.

Assess the situation.

What factors have come into play to distract
you from your daily practice?

What changes need to be made to accommodate
life with your practice?

Is a small respite necessary? If so, determine
what is needed.

Make an agreement when you will return to
your practice.

Have compassion and optimism for your moment
of disconnection.

Discern options for avoiding new disruptions
in the future.

How do you maintain the course of being a better
person from now to forevermore?

With love and compassion for every next step you
make and for every one that is not taken.

With frequent visits to the great within for
assistance, guidance, and ancient wisdom.

With gratitude for all the memories of times
when you have demonstrated the better person
that you are.

With the help of all those who read this book and broached the challenges of becoming a better person, as did you.

With the help of all those who stand with you, even when you are unaware of their presence.

With acceptance that you are a good person, who is becoming better every day.

With faith that you are loved and cherished just as you are.

Dear Reader, the time is now. Throughout your lifetime, which is far more expansive than you remember, you have always sought to be a better person. It is simply who you are. Hopefully, *Seeking A Better Me* has reminded you of the innate qualities that lie within you. You are the Better Person that you seek, but unfortunately, that truth is often forgotten as one lives his or her busy life.

However, when we take time to explore our true self, the truth is once again revealed. This never-ending process of exploring, discovering, and remembering who we really are inspires us to strive harder to become more than we think we are in the moment. The sweet moments of realization that surface during our excursions of Self propel us further into the possibilities that yet await us. We are forever seeking more and as we seek more, we become more. Each new awareness reminds us that the ongoing process is essential to our evolutionary development, our fulfillment of the eternal life experience that we are granted.

We are the more that we seek, and we are also more than we appear to be, more than we can possibly imagine. We are all this, and we are more.

This is the beautiful Self that you really are. Keep seeking, Dear Friend, for you are constantly becoming the Better Person that you seek.

...In peace be and safe travels...

About the Author

As you read this book and others presented by Claudia Helt, the purpose of her role will become clear. Claudia's personal life has been one of ordinary circumstances. She grew up in a small town, attended university attaining two degrees in Psychology, and then enjoyed over three decades working as a psychotherapist.

She was, as you might imagine, initially taken aback when she began hearing a Voice of an unseen Presence. For her, the manner in which she receives these communiques is as mysterious as the material itself; however, after two decades of participating in this process, she now simply accepts these experiences as cherished connections for which she is eternally grateful.

Even after all these years her commitment to this collaborative process remains firm, and she intends to continue sharing future communiques as she is invited and guided.

All books can be easily purchased through:

The Center for Peaceful Transitions
www.centerforpeacefultransitions.com

Balboa Press
www.balboapress.com

Amazon.com
www.amazon.com

Printed in the United States
by Baker & Taylor Publisher Services